We all have a voice that needs to be heard.

VoiceThreading

VoiceThreading

TESOL Strategy Guide

DAVID KENT

Pedagogy Press

National Library of Australia Cataloguing-in-Publication entry:
Kent, David Bradley, author.
VoiceThreading / David Kent.

ISBN: 9781925555035 (paperback) (5)
TESOL strategy guide ; 5.
Includes bibliographical references.
Teachers of English to Speakers of Other Languages.
Educational technology
Teaching-Aids and devices.
Teachers—Training of.
Internet in education.
English language—Study and teaching—Foreign speakers.

Pedagogy Press. Sydney, Australia.
www.pedagogypress.com

First Edition.

For teachers everywhere.

CONTENTS

Preface

This *TESOL Strategy Guide*, number five in the set, arose out of the clear need to provide teacher training and a means of professional development to educators living and working in the Republic of Korea. Many expatriate English language instructors have arrived in-country without training as a teacher or educator, and are often left to take care of their own professional development while engaged in teaching English to speakers of other languages (TESOL). As many of these teachers come to enjoy working as expatriates, they often begin to seek out their own professional development on topics that they wish to learn more about, on skills that they wish to gain, and on techniques that they wish to integrate within their classrooms. It is this need, which is common to all teachers of English in all contexts around the globe, that this book seeks to fill.

Organization of the text

Each *TESOL Strategy Guide* can be read standalone or in conjunction with others from the set. Each book provides information on a technology topic, and has been designed around a question-based format similar to the following:

- Overview
- What is … ?
- How can I use … ?
- What types of … exist?
- What elements are behind an effective … ?
- How can … lend itself to TESOL?
- How can I start using … with students?
- How do I evaluate a … ?
- What tools are available for … creation?
- How do I craft a … ?
- How would I use a tool to create a … ?
- What are the key points behind … use in the TESOL context?

A comprehensive list of resources with links to pertinent web sites and applications is included, along with lesson plan guides, example implementation techniques, and various free to use handouts for the teacher and student alike. A reference list of all works cited also allows those teachers with an interest in a particular topic to engage in reading further on the issues that most interest them and impact their learners.

It is hoped that this book will provide both education and something new for all teachers – be they trained or untrained, pre-service, in-service, seasoned, or retired.

1

Overview

VoiceThread firmly establishes itself as a tool that has the exciting potential to give an actual audible voice to those language students who rarely, if ever, speak the target language in class, and it does so by providing students with the means to construct visually-based digital conversations. In light of this, the pedagogical affordances provided by this web-based tool are considered within this book, along with the types of educational VoiceThreads that are in use today. The efficacy behind VoiceThread development, with and for students, is then oriented toward the teaching of English to speakers of other languages (TESOL) with a brief overview of VoiceThread instructional strategies that are suited to second-language learners of English, supported by example activities and resources. A means of evaluating language production and learning outcomes afforded through use of the tool then follows, along with an overview of the techniques essential for monitoring, producing, and guiding effective VoiceThread development among language learners. A tutorial for getting started with the technology, and developing visually-based digital conversations, is also provided, along with a variety of other useful resources to assist students and teachers as they begin to participate in VoiceThreading.

2
What is VoiceThread?

VoiceThread is an asynchronous online tool and associated mobile application that employs uploaded audio comments, a narrating tool, text balloons, and web-cam video annotation to support the online discussion of media artifacts. These media artifacts can consist of documents, images, presentations or videos. The tool allows for moderated feedback, which in turn allows both instructors and students to control the dissemination of feedback in terms of monitoring postings for inappropriate content. Most importantly, after creation, VoiceThreads are immediately web-accessible and can be embedded into other websites including blogs, wikis, and course management systems like Moodle, thereby supporting student accessibility across a range of platforms (Pacansky-Brock, 2013). To date, VoiceThread has proved useful in a number of educational contexts from second language learning (Bush, 2009; Akasha, 2011; Pallos & Pallos, 2011; Sun, Yu, & Gao, 2013) to literacy development (Smith & Dobson, 2009) as well as in use with adults and young learners alike (Gillis, Luthin, Parette, & Blum, 2012; Lewis, Burks, Shumack & Shumack, 2014).

VoiceThread was originally launched in 2007, and today, it allows for navigation between slides and comment postings in five different ways: using voice with a microphone, using voice by telephone, typing text, uploading an audio file, or by making a webcam video. Postings can be augmented with the use of a narration drawing tool during the recording process. Any created VoiceThread can then be shared with friends, groups of learners or colleagues, and they in turn can leave comments on the thread or edit it (if the necessary permissions allow).

3

How can I use VoiceThread?

VoiceThread was not specifically designed to be used as an educational tool, and while the functionality of a number of the applications features do not always marry with pedagogy, it is possible to match many VoiceThread features with pedagogical affordances (Burden & Atkinson, 2008), including:

- focusing learner attention on specifics via the zoom tool;
- providing formative feedback on media related content emerging from asynchronous comments pertaining to thread artifact(s);
- learner communities can visualize and provide responses to cumulative postings, as users can post comments reflecting on other users comments;
- instant feedback can be provided from a potentially global audience, as the thread can be made viewable by anyone online;
- comment moderation, which allows the thread to be managed and monitored for appropriateness; and
- an 'at once' visual overview of content (rather rather than a long text-based thread) which

stems from capturing a full discussion on a single page.

The VoiceThread context also affords students with an environment from which to work collaboratively to communicate and engage in learning, while teachers can utilize the tool for creation, discussion, assessment, or even in a flipped classroom context (Hughes, 2012; Nicholson, 2013; Moore, Gillet & Steele, 2014).

VoiceThreads provide a creative outlet for students that encourages idea sharing, and this can potentially allow students to learn more about others' experiences and views as they explore the thinking of others through images, text, use of narration drawing tools, and voice. Instead of the traditional, which may be full of teacher-talk or conversations on a turn-by-turn basis, VoiceThreads can maintain multiple discussion strands, and as responses can be made asynchronously, learners have more time to absorb each strand and develop more complex thought out responses to each of them. VoiceThreads make it easy to see what students contribute and how much effort they put into producing the comments that they create. In turn, these comments allow teachers to see if students understand the key concepts that are being studied, as learners begin to put things into their own words and make comments on peers and teacher VoiceThread content and contributions. As a result, many different types of VoiceThread have emerged.

The extensive use of VoiceThread by educators today has prompted the emergence of a significant research base around the use of the tool, as well as sites like the Voicethread 4 Education wiki to emerge. This wiki has come to provide a library of VoiceThread examples from which to gather potential pedagogical uses and ideas, along with examples of best practice.

4

What type of educational VoiceThreads exist?

As VoiceThreads can be used to share information, start discussions, receive feedback, or simply tell a story, Poelzer (2009) along with Elwood (2010) recognize the educational opportunities that VoiceThread can provide, and the strategies required for its effective use as a learning tool – particularly for the creation of digital storytelling projects, demonstrating knowledge gained in research or inquiry projects, documenting student progress over time, and sharing information with an authentic audience. Poelzer also views VoiceThread as extremely adaptable, and as useful for a multitude of purposes across a range of subjects and curriculums, as numerous subject areas can be integrated within a single VoiceThread which, as Dyck (2007) points out, can be used to develop storytelling and deep thinking skills, as well as communication skills, or even used as a means to conduct assessment. A number of different types of VoiceThread use by educators has emerged (Pires, 2010), including:

- collaborative digital storytelling creation,
- discussion, suggestion, and opinion activities,
- problem solving skill development tasks,
- peer review,
- keyword identification,
- image notation and captioning,
- revision work completion,
- book and movie review development,
- digital portfolio construction,
- as well as comic strip building.

Burden and Atkinson (2008) also identify a number of activities suitable for VoiceThread use, from stimulus, narrative, collaborative, conceptual, empathic, and representational. Such as:

- video posting without sound, with learners commenting on what might be being said;
- presenting the first half of a video clip, and then asking learners to predict what might happen next; or

- assigning different roles to students, and having them post comments assuming the perspectives of that role.

Going one step further, Vesper (2008) provides a series of examples of effective practice that includes using VoiceThread as a tool to extend the literacy and numeracy skills of students; allow for the showcasing and evaluation of student work; develop collaborative skills amongst students; and provide for the career building options of teachers. Student literacy skills can be developed by presenting written texts in oral form, creating poetry anthologies and book reviews, constructing choose-your-own-adventure stories (which can be augmented with student generated artwork, with narration and text, to extend the creativity and collaboration aspects), writing stories to go with images, exploring 'what if' variations of video clips, and creating instructions or showing the steps in a process to match media artifacts. Numeracy skills can be enhanced through development of math games and problem solving puzzles, focusing on real life problem solving situations, and representing mathematical concepts visually. Showcasing and evaluating work can be achieved by preparing digital portfolios and goal setting, while taking part in collaborative projects involves students' thinking around topics, and providing commentary and debate on the issues, and then summarizing class discussions and research within a VoiceThread. Career building for teachers can also occur with VoiceThread by allowing teachers to house and provide classroom teaching content for students, engage in the delivery of professional development, and share ideas between colleagues and then critically reflect on aspects of the ideas presented.

5

What elements are behind an effective VoiceThread?

If you are new to VoiceThreading, then to see what constitutes the creation of an effective VoiceThread, you can begin by experimenting. You could start out by commenting on a few existing VoiceThreads before creating a couple of practice threads yourself. After viewing several, and leaving a comment or two here and there, start by creating a VoiceThread that is small, contains only a few artifacts, and focuses on a single activity or topic.

Creating an initial VoiceThread should begin with an understanding of the direction in which you wish to take it. After that, media artifacts should be selected that will promote or lead the VoiceThread in this direction. Also, when creating a VoiceThread as an example for students, provide model comments. This is particularly important as many students need examples so that they know what is expected of them when making their comments and replies. Just be sure to select and prepare content so that it is engaging and will lead to potential interaction. See the resource notes on incorporating and constructing a VoiceThread in Chapter 14 for an overview to follow in initial VoiceThread construction for classroom use.

If you intend to have students create their own VoiceThreads, then be sure to provide topics that allow room for student creativity to emerge, as this can lead to more thoughtful and interesting comments. Keep pedagogy in mind, and ensure that a solid learning outcome can develop from student participation and involvement with the VoiceThread process. It may prove best to start students off in pairs or groups, as this can help promote brainstorming and prove effective for them to draft any initial comments for the associated topic they have chosen or been provided. This also helps ensure that the very first comments that students produce follow the intention of the VoiceThread, and are on topic and well thought out, particularly since they are composed with teacher assistance. It also ensures that all students have, at the very least, one comment to place on their VoiceThread and, as such, can become familiar with the basic means of the commenting process. This also encourages students with low in-class participation to begin to contribute equally to the project. However, perhaps limit initial participation to a small group for each thread, as this can later be expanded as students become used to the site and get better at moderating comments and filtering content. If so desired, the VoiceThread can then be opened up to other users and stakeholders such as parents, and if the teaching context allows for it, it can be open to anyone at all, as this can provide potential incoming comments containing naturally spoken language from a global audience.

After students have created their own VoiceThreads, it is important that you become involved in each one. Ensure that you are invited to every student-created VoiceThread so that you can provide any necessary guidance, advice, structure, or authority and most importantly, monitor development and provide filtering. Don't just leave the provision of comments up to the students; keep modeling appropriate content for students to mirror by focusing on style, structure, language use, grammar, length, and anything else that you may consider to be an important aspect to tailor for that particular class or group of students. To further assist in generating appropriate and effective student comments, it may prove necessary to enforce guidelines which will guarantee that student participation is controlled and secured by structuring expected content. Continuously aim to provide teacher direction, but also maintain a student-centered learning environment through the promotion of student autonomy. Assist learners in identifying content and comments that are inappropriate, and be sure to monitor all comments so that any inappropriate content can be filtered out immediately. Establish an expected standard of quality, and assist students in being able to reach that level. Hold students accountable for their online work, and help them to truly understand that the work they create is going out to a wider audience than just the classroom teacher and their classmates, and that it is work that can be accessed at any time (not just during class or school hours).

It is also advisable to spotlight student comments. This allows teachers to reinforce comments that are effective and stimulate the growth of a VoiceThread, and to see that students produce comments that stick to the main topic of the thread. Spotlighting can also empower learners and spur motivation while highlighting material that students are expected to produce. Poor comments can prove to be effective examples to highlight, where comments that might be considered 'throw away', or ones that students make to just fulfill the commenting task are targeted. This can drive home the notion that such comments that are meaningless are both unconstructive and are not useful or highly valued in digital spaces (Hoskins Sakamoto, 2010). That said, when highlighting poor comments, it is also important to indicate how these comments can best be improved.

Several other factors to consider include: access, paid account use, stable hardware and internet connections, reliance on reusable content, and practicing the safe-guarding of students.

The means by which your classroom provides access to computers and the internet will largely dictate the possibilities of VoiceThread use. Some teachers may have a single computer in the room which is tied to an interactive whiteboard or beam projector. Other teachers may have to schedule computer lab time at their school before they can gain access to computers for student use, while other students may only be able to access computers at home and not at all in the teaching context.

If using a paid account, a number of teacher aliases can be created under the one account and this can assist in monitoring students and grouping them with ease. However, paid accounts can prove to be expensive, even those that are 'educator priced', and you should be sure that VoiceThread is a technology that you consider actually worth your own personal investment if paying out-of-pocket.

Also keep in mind that VoiceThreads are an online dependent technology, and must be accessed with a reliable internet connection from a computer or table device that is capable of accessing the internet efficiently. In relation to this, you must prepare a contingency plan to cover any internet outage or technological breakdowns if you are to use VoiceThread in the classroom during work hours. This notion also ties into the need to ensure that the hardware to be used must be in good working order and accessible at the appropriate times – for example, by confirming computer lab bookings or in a bring-your-own-device (BYOD) setting confirm that the devices are actually brought to school. Students must also have access to any planned data that they will use to create their VoiceThreads, and carrying this on a USB stick or being able to access it from a shared folder on a network or other computer is necessary.

Further, you shouldn't be reinventing the wheel each time that you start a VoiceThread project. Previously created VoiceThreads can be used over and over again, and examples of student created work can be saved or exported as examples of best practice. With this in mind, copyright issues are also important. Students may need to be reminded or taught about aspects of educational fair use as well as plagiarism. This is especially true of young learners, but even of some adults. It may prove necessary to provide a citation or reference list in a word file on the last slide of each VoiceThread that students create, even if only for the sake of practice.

Finally, always safeguard students, and constantly monitor all student-created VoiceThreads for inappropriate content and/or comments. Further, ensure that young learners do not upload photographs of themselves or use their full names, or any private personal data when making comments. In this regard, students in the English as a foreign language (EFL) context may prove better off using their English nicknames when working with VoiceThread projects. So too, in some teaching contexts, it will be necessary to gain parent permission before students can participate in any use of a VoiceThread.

6

How can VoiceThread lend itself to TESOL?

A number of possibilities exist for utilizing VoiceThread in the teaching of English to speakers of other languages. Students can participate in speaking and listening activities when recording or responding to a VoiceThread; teachers can set topic-based presentations or dialog-based conversational tasks; and classes can share projects with other classes, allowing them to see what other students are studying and to provide comments on that group of learners who then respond in turn. It also allows students to provide a window into their experiences and ideas, and it allows stakeholders (administrators, teachers, parents, and the students themselves) to monitor the learning outcomes and the educational product that emerges.

As the VoiceThread website (VoiceThread, 2016) itself states that 'participation is not optional', it appears that VoiceThread has established itself as a tool that any EFL educator can immediately recognize as having the exciting potential that gives an actual audible voice to those students who rarely, or if ever, speak in class. It also provides a voice for those unwilling to speak out in front of peers, and if such students still feel too uncomfortable to actually verbalize their thoughts or responses in a second language, then they can always retain the option to type comments. As such, if the focus of the lesson is on speaking and pronunciation, as it is many times in the language classroom, then you may inform students that they can use any option but the keyboard to comment. Leaving spoken comments on a VoiceThread can break down the affective filters that many learners carry with them into language classrooms (Hacker, 2010). On the other hand, if the focus is on reading and writing, then students can limit their comments to writing and notation if deemed necessary.

In this respect, for English language learners, VoiceThread comes to afford a number of opportunities to engage in online discussion while practicing speaking and writing skills asynchronously. This comes to support a multiple intelligence approach to learning and helps encourage participation and build learner confidence by providing time for students to reflect and construct responses before posting (Recchio-Demmin, 2009).

7

How can I start using VoiceThread with students?

An important resource that is introduced in Chapter 3, and one where TESOL educators can gain insight into the myriad uses of VoiceThread in education, is that provided by Cassinelli (2016). The VoiceThread 4 education wiki provides an extremely comprehensive collection of examples from educators and instructors of all ages and academic backgrounds, including those from the K-12 environment, the tertiary education sector, special education, and the English as a foreign language (EFL) and English as a second language (ESL) context. A few examples, with extension ideas, from that web site include creating discussions based on themes or genres (such as emotions or music), allowing students to introduce their hometowns, countries, or even themselves and their family in a VoiceThread, as well as creating an international collaborative project based on food image postings – with students from one country inviting students from other countries to comment on food images and provide recipes and their own food postings as well. VoiceThreads can also be useful in teaching the alphabet to young learners. Hoskins Sakamoto (2010) has applied VoiceThread to make an alphabet book which has a photo for each letter, and students make the letter shapes with their bodies. The pages also contain audio comments from students as they pronounce each letter and match it to an English word, for example, 'a, a, apple; b, b, bird'. The 'book' can be exported and provided to students at the end of the alphabet, so they each have a personal copy of the project. Such a project can prove valuable for extending lesson outcomes as it allows for other teachers and students around the world to comment on each of the 'letter' pages. Students can therefore gain increased exposure to a range of different native and non-native English speaking accents as well as providing teaching opportunities associated with speaker country of origin, and perhaps also vocabulary. Such a project would be a common one in EFL and ESL classrooms alike, and through the use of VoiceThread, opportunities exist for comments to be made from children in native-English speaking countries. Such children can also produce their own alphabet book in response, or provide more vocabulary for each letter. So too, parents can be provided with the link so that the material can be practiced at home for reinforcement.

In fact, almost any classroom content can be ported to a VoiceThread context for use as a potential language learning activity. VoiceThread is particularly well-suited as a means from which students can introduce themselves using images, videos, and text excerpts of favorite books or poems, as well as providing details of their hobbies, background information on their friends, family, pets, and even their favorite places to relax or to go on vacation. Other traditional activity uses of VoiceThread can include focusing students on a single topic by having them present on popular social issues or issues of interest to them, providing a book or film review, or using it to tell a progressive 'Chinese whisper' type story. In such a story, the teacher begins by adding an initial image to a VoiceThread and making the first comment, with the students in turn adding their images and comments to extend the story, and the teacher adding a final image and a closing comment. Other VoiceThreads containing images may be set up to allow students to extract information from the photographs presented by asking *wh*-questions (Who? What? When? Where? Why? How?). To expand the deeper thinking skills of students, they can then be directed to focus on examining the images in more detail, and commenting on what influences may have impacted upon elements in the image when it was taken, and how these relate to the world today. Such a process can also assist in helping students gain the language skills required to tell complex stories through the use of picture and narration. Taking the theme of thinking skills one step further, clue-based games may be developed with one group of students preparing an image montage that can be uploaded to a VoiceThread to provide hints for a question or riddle that students ask as a comment. Other students can then make their own comment on the VoiceThread to guess the answer to the riddle, before uploading their own hint montage and riddle. Answers can then be provided in class, or by making an answer comment at a set date or on the final slide of the VoiceThread so that the solution can be discovered at any time.

Other potentially exciting uses of VoiceThread involve employing it to teach directions, housing dialog-based language learning activities, or using the mandated textbook more creatively. In teaching directions, images can be zoomed in on and panned around freely, and this allows for various directions to be stated and followed with ease. An image of a map can be uploaded to the VoiceThread with a teacher comment asking for directions (for example How do I get to the supermarket?). This initial comment should be followed by an example model comment, illustrating how to get to the supermarket and any special vocabulary (Go straight for two blocks then take a right, continue straight, and you'll see the supermarket on the left). Further, when housing dialog-based language learning activities, a

VoiceThread can be set up with an initial image to provide an overview of the topic or language situation presented. Students can then engage in a conversational turn-taking dialog. For example, a picture of a restaurant can be uploaded with two students engaging in a conversation as waiter and customer, with images and comments uploaded to suit the progression of the topic as the conversation evolves. Alternatively, as the conversation evolves, other students can take over the turn-taking process. In this case, a second pair of students acting as the same waiter and customer could then add a menu image with the customer asking for advice on what to order or asking for more details about a certain dish. A third pair may continue the waiter-customer dialog by experiencing a problem (such as a fly in the soup) or simply asking for and paying the bill. Where a pre-selected textbook must be used and followed meticulously over a preplanned course of study (as is the case in many middle and high schools), parts of the textbook can be scanned by teachers and inserted into a VoiceThread so that students can provide spoken answers to the questions that are asked in the text. This technique can also be augmented so that students can complete any associated textbook homework on lesson content via a single VoiceThread, with this VoiceThread then coming to serve as an assessment e-portfolio tool.

8

How do I evaluate a VoiceThread?

For VoiceThreads, the rubric presented to students for evaluation should take into account the two sides of student participation – the creation, development, and end-product that is ultimately produced by the learner or their group, which is the VoiceThread itself, as well as the various comments made on other class members' VoiceThreads. As always, rubrics should be provided to learners beforehand so that they understand what will actually be assessed, and allowing them to ask questions about what is being assessed if they don't understand the rubric.

Evaluation rubrics, particularly those using indicators across several categories, are essential when assessing the quality of student work on any complex multimedia-based project. Although it is useful for the busy teacher to apply pre-made rubrics, it is even better if teachers formulate their own. Such rubrics can reflect their teaching environment and the points that they wish to assess. One good source for this is

Rubistar, where there are a number of pre-made evaluation options as well as information on how to create unique context sensitive evaluation instruments. The rubrics section of the resources list also contains several other rubric creation tools that may prove worthwhile to look over.

Following are two sample rubrics that can be used with students in any classroom, including those participating in VoiceThread production from within the TESOL setting. One rubric focuses on the VoiceThread itself, in terms of student construction and development, and the other focuses on the student replies and comments to VoiceThreads created by their peers.

The rating scale used in the following rubrics go from 1 to 5, with 1 being poor, 2 fair, 3 average, 4 good, and 5 excellent. 'Average' is used as a midpoint so that students can see how each particular skill relates to peers. This allows teachers to identify those skills that are weak in individual students, and those that may need improvement.

VoiceThreads

Assessment Item	Assessment Criteria	Score
Media	Selection of artifacts reflects topic, helps support viewpoint of content (source credited where appropriate).	1 2 3 4 5
Content	Well researched and supported information relevant to topic is provided in an organized fashion (sources credited where appropriate).	1 2 3 4 5
Thread Quality	Images are clear, video is not blurry, volume is loud enough so that the voice of speakers is consistently audible.	1 2 3 4 5
Notation Tool	The tool is used to highlight when necessary, and is not used in a manner that is distracting.	1 2 3 4 5
Collaboration (if appropriate)	Students/groups divided workload fairly, and undertook VoiceThread completion cooperatively.	1 2 3 4 5
Language Skills	Language use contributes to topic clarity, style, and development (e.g., appropriate vocabulary selected, consistent spelling and grammar).	1 2 3 4 5

Comments

Assessment Item	Assessment Criteria	Score
Focus	Comments are directed to topic, stay on topic, and are more than a few words.	1 2 3 4 5
Understanding	Comments show clear understanding of topic and others' comments.	1 2 3 4 5
Accuracy	Comments are accurate and contain no errors regarding the topic, and clearly reflect thought and preparation.	1 2 3 4 5
Notation Tool	The tool is used to highlight points, and not for its own sake.	1 2 3 4 5
Language Skills	No spelling or grammar inconsistency in text-based comments, spoken comments free of superfluous wording and are more spontaneous than scripted in appearance.	1 2 3 4 5

Ratings: 1 Poor 2 Fair 3 Average 4 Good 5 Excellent

9

How do I get started with VoiceThread development?

After registering with the VoiceThread website and having a contact list of students, you will need to create you first active VoiceThread for use with classes. Initially, select an issue that maintains a focus on obtaining the desired outcome of a lesson or topic. For example, you may simply want the VoiceThread to give a voice to students who don't speak out in the classroom, or you may want the VoiceThread to promote discussion of a topic, or even to have it act as a turn-taking slideshow to promote a dialog-based language activity, a story, or even a student generated narrative.

A good place to start with initial development would be preparing the necessary media or content for use in the VoiceThread before planning what comments to provide alongside the presented content. This step would also involve developing initial comments that are short (one to three sentences perhaps), as longer comments may discourage learners (particularly beginner second-language students) who may reconsider their ability to leave a comment. This would be followed by ordering content so that scaffolded learning can be provided in a teacher-directed manner, but in a way that still focuses on providing content that maintains a student-centered approach to the use and access content that is presented and contained within the VoiceThread. To be successful in this endeavor, it is important to focus on developing a VoiceThread based on well storyboarded material and comments that inspire learners to add media artifacts and respond to your and others' comments so that the VoiceThread can grow. Chapter 14 contains a guide and resource notes that can assist in any initial VoiceThread construction and implementation, and it is designed primarily for teacher use. A similar VoiceThread creation handout which is oriented more toward student use, along with associated resource notes, is also provided in the same chapter. The use of this handout in the classroom can also be extended with the VoiceThread comment reflection extension activity handout, which follows it in Chapter 14. The reflection/extension activity can be used to prompt student thinking on comments, or used in a follow-up lesson that centers around a discussion of the comments that students found users left on their VoiceThreads. In either case, the reflection handout should enable learners to record items of interest, factors that they agreed or disagreed with, things that changed their thinking, elements that challenged them, and, along with language learning outcomes (such as new vocabulary or expressions that they were able to employ or pickup), things that they learned from engaging in VoiceThread use.

10

How do I encourage the growth of a VoiceThread?

After creating an active VoiceThread, and providing a link or sending out invites to students, all VoiceThreads will need to be nurtured. Three ways to do this are illustrated by Ferriter (2010), and are related to the following elements: viewing and thinking about the VoiceThread, leaving a succinct spoken or written comment, and leaving an effective spoken or written comment that promotes future participation. Although these elements are necessary in any VoiceThread, some targeting is required for the teaching of English to speakers of other languages (TESOL) context as detailed in the following sections.

1. Viewing and thinking about the VoiceThread

Students will need to examine the content of the VoiceThread, listening to and reading each of the comments by previous users (if any). To encourage active listening, to promote writing skills, and to develop thinking skills while stimulating interactive involvement in the language learning process, students should collect, connect, question, and express.

Collect

While viewing the VoiceThread for the first time, students should collect their thoughts about the information presented, particularly anything that is interesting or new to them (including vocabulary or expressions), and write down this information in point form.

Connect

It is important to emphasize that students should attempt to connect the incoming information from the VoiceThread and associated comments with preexisting schema, and that they should build upon their existing language skills.

Question

Students should be encouraged to ask questions about the VoiceThread that they are viewing. Is there anything that is confusing? Is there language or content that is unfamiliar?

Express
Students might need help with being creative with their language use. Support students in their judgments.

2. Leaving a succinct spoken or written comment
In the teaching of English to speakers of other languages (TESOL), it may be wise to provide students with a series of set phrases to get comments started, and setting a sentence or word limit for their responses. Almost any conversation starter expression could be used to help students leave comments, particularly those from students' current textbooks. Even some idiomatic expressions can also be introduced – for example:

I remember a time …
I once heard …
On the other hand …
I wouldn't be caught …

3. Leaving an effective spoken or written comment

Learners of any sort, and perhaps even teachers too, might also need some general advice regarding commenting and responding. This is especially true if the comments are to promote critical thinking, new language use, and promote further participation and interactivity.

Repeat/rephrase

Restate part of a previous comment or the content that garners attention.

Detail

Put thoughts into words or text as concisely as possible. What exactly are you students thinking?

Elaborate

Make an exact point, or complete the language learning objective, while attempting to use new expressions or vocabulary gained from the VoiceThread.

Create

Spur the thinking of future commenters by providing a memorable finish to comments. One strategy may be ending comments with a rhetorical question or by leaving a quote as a summary. Comments need to be closed in a manner that helps to spur conversation.

It is important to ensure that students are prepared to have other people respond to their comments in both a negative and positive manner. If learners receive a negative response, they first and foremost need to accept the criticism and not be offended. Help them learn to use any response as an opportunity to gain feedback and an understanding of others' opinions and ideas, and as a means to improve upon their language skills. Second, ensure that students take the time to properly organize their thoughts so that they can respond to any comments in a constructive manner. Time to compose responses is one of the biggest advantages afforded by asynchronous communication. Also, as the internet and VoiceThreads are potentially open to the public, and can remain a matter of public record until the

VoiceThread owner deletes the thread, you should ensure that students are responding appropriately and in ways conducive to their language learning.

11

How would I create and house a VoiceThread?

Like many software tools and web sites, the VoiceThread website works by stepping users through a wizard so that a VoiceThread can be created simply in only a few steps. However, before you can start creating a VoiceThread and before your students can start commenting and creating as well, you first have to register with the website. It's free, and it creates an account specific to you to house the VoiceThreads that you create, and it gives you quick access to the VoiceThreads that you have subscribed to. This walkthrough explains the process through use of the VoiceThread website which is accessible via an internet-based browser. The process using the Android or iOS-based application is similar.

Step One – Starting out:

Signing in

Go to the VoiceThread website, then click on either 'Sign in' or 'Register'. If you are a new user, you will have to sign in, after which you'll then see the basic account navigation page. Other paid account options, with their own special features, are also available (K-12, Higher Ed, Business, and PRO), but these won't be discussed here.

Step Two – Navigating:

The welcome page

The most important tabs on the initial navigation page are 'Browse', 'Create', and 'Home'. Clicking the 'Browse' tab will bring up all the VoiceThreads that authors have chosen to be available for browsing. After you create a VoiceThread, you will be given the option to include it under this section, or you may wish to disclude it for increased privacy, particularly if you are creating VoiceThreads with students and are not paying for one of the educational platforms available. The 'Create' tab is the place to start when wanting to make a new VoiceThread, after which you will find the created thread housed under the initial page that greets you after log in – the 'Home' screen. This section presents you with a thumbnail view of all the VoiceThreads that you have created, ones that you've been invited to view, and others that you have chosen to subscribe to. Any small yellow quote bubble over a VoiceThread indicates that the thread has unread comments.

Step Three – Creating your VoiceThread:
Uploading content
To begin, click on the 'Create' tab from the main page after signing into your VoiceThread account, then click on the 'Add media' button or drag and drop files into the browser window for upload. You will then be able to upload a variety of media artifacts from a number of sources, but do keep in mind that single file sizes are limited to 25 MB for free accounts and 100 MB for paid accounts. Media choices may include pre-prepared documents (DOC, DOCX, ODS, ODT, PDF, XLS, XLSX), graphics (BMP, GIF, JPEG, PNG), presentation files (ODP, PDF, PPT, PPTX), movie files (AVI, FLV, quicktime, WMV – depending on the

codec, with H.264 preferred), or with paid accounts sound files such as MP3 or WAV format for uploading prerecorded comments. Source options for media files include uploading directly from your computer, selecting sources by URL (uniform resource locator, or web page address), recording direct from your webcam or from a number of other internet-based services. These other internet-based services include: accessing any images from VoiceThreads appearing on your 'Home' screen, grabbing photos from your Flickr account, accessing photos from your FaceBook account, as well as providing access to the Khan Academy and free images available from the New York Public Library. Essentially, any number of items can be imported into a single VoiceThread, and you can always return to a VoiceThread to add more items or more slides, or even come back to rearrange the content that has already been imported. Just remember, when using a free account, you will be limited to creating only three VoiceThreads, but of course these can be deleted and new ones created as necessary, or you may even choose to export them (for a fee). Of note, formats that will not be accepted at all for upload include: html, SWF, TXT, and ZIP.

Step Four – Marking up the VoiceThread:
Leaving comments

The process of commenting is the same for any registered user, from teachers and students to the general public. To leave a comment on your VoiceThread, or any VoiceThread for that matter, first select the slide that you want to make a comment on by clicking on the left or right arrows to navigate to the slide you want. Alternatively, you can click on the 'Slide' button to bring up a thumbnail view of each slide in the VoiceThread, and click directly on the image of the slide that you want to leave a comment upon. Once you are at the slide that you wish to comment on, several commenting options become available on the comment panel after clicking the 'Comment' button. You can record a voice comment by telephone, or record a video comment using your web camera. You can also record a voice comment by microphone, or simply type a text-based comment with your keyboard. A prerecorded MP3 or wav file can be uploaded, but only if you have access to a paid account. After making a comment, it can be previewed before being saved on the VoiceThread slide. In addition, a notation function is available when recording a comment. The notation function provides access to a pen that allows doodling over the slide, and is controlled by the mouse. The color of the notation can be changed from the default white if desired, and can be rendered brighter or duller as necessary. Each time that you leave a comment on a VoiceThread, a thumbnail of your personal icon will appear to the left or right side of that particular slide. People will then be able to interact with your comment by clicking on your image. Underneath the VoiceThread is a comment line that graphically illustrates the length of the time each comment will take to play, and this can also be used to navigate amongst comments and play them back in any order, rather than letting them play sequentially.

Step Five – Publishing your VoiceThread:
Sharing options

Publishing your VoiceThread involves setting viewing options, managing the distribution of the thread, and then obtaining a distributable link. Once you've uploaded the desired content to your VoiceThread and made any appropriate comments, you will be at the 'Share' stage. To ensure that your VoiceThread will be viewable by more people than just you, it is important to click on the 'Options' button. This step is also important for ethical reasons, as it is here that you can ensure that suitable choices are made regarding student privacy. Publishing options include: allowing anyone to view the thread, or only those designated (recommended for school age use); allow anyone to comment (recommended), or no comments accepted; allow comments to appear immediately, or approve comments before they are visible to others (recommended); and the VoiceThread is viewable by all in the 'Browse' section, or the VoiceThread will not appear in the 'Browse' section of the VoiceThread home page (recommended). You may of course decide on the options appropriate for your teaching context, but these suggestions would work for many educators. Just keep in mind that VoiceThreads that appear on the 'Browse' page are also viewable and indexed by other sites such as search engines like Google. After saving the publishing options, you can click on the 'Get a Link' button so that the VoiceThread Share URL can be copied to the computer's clipboard. The link can now be pasted into an email for distribution.

Step Six – VoiceThreading one step further: Embedding, playing back, or exporting

After creating your VoiceThread, and sending out a share URL by email or other means, you may also want to consider embedding the thread into the school learner management system (LMS) or your own personal website, fine-tuning playback options, or exporting the thread. After clicking the 'Options' button, playback can be refined in the following manner:

- by setting timing options (in seconds) before each slide moves on to the next (four or five seconds is recommended);

- start playing when opened (recommended);
- don't allow commenters to delete their own comments (not recommended); and
- allow others to export (not recommended).

Exporting is available by clicking the 'Export' tab after clicking 'Share'. It is an excellent feature if you wish to archive your VoiceThread along with the comments and notations made on it, or even if you just wish to share it in an offline context. A number of exports are allowed for those who have upgraded their account, but this is not the case for free accounts where a small fee is charged per exported VoiceThread. Embedding the VoiceThread, or to gain access to the code required to embed the VoiceThread, is available after clicking the 'Embed' button. The code can then be copied for use with your own personal site, or school LMS such as Moodle. Alternatively, the VoiceThread can be posted directly to notable social media sites, such as Facebook and Twitter.

Step Seven – Inviting users to comment:

Setting permissions

Inviting users, or students, to comment on your VoiceThread is essential – particularly when teaching English to speakers of other languages. The VoiceThread link can be obtained by clicking 'Share', and to ensure others can comment on the VoiceThread, the 'Allow anyone to view' and 'Allow anyone to comment' options should be selected. Educators who can afford it may prefer opting for paid accounts as it can be a little easier in registering students and keeping them grouped under your own account and by classes, and also to work with VoiceThreads in a more secure environment. Nonetheless, for those educators who choose to provide a direct link to a VoiceThread, learners can then start to leave comments only after each has have registered as a user on the site.

Step Eight – Finalizing:

Finding your VoiceThread and turning it into reusable content

After you have created a VoiceThread, set up publishing options, and invited people to comment on it, you will then be able to gain access to it from the 'Home' screen after logging into VoiceThread. The 'Home' screen houses all the VoiceThreads that you have created, as well as others (such as ones that you have subscribed to). Each of the VoiceThreads has several options associated with it when you move your mouse over it. For all VoiceThreads, you can 'Share', or 'Remove' the VoiceThread, or identify how many views it has seen and how many comments have been left on it. Options for those that you have created include: 'Delete' to erase the thread, 'Make a copy' to duplicate the thread, 'Edit' to change the thread, or 'Share' to distribute the thread. The 'Make copy' function can prove invaluable as it allows you to duplicate the VoiceThread with 'Just your comments', with 'All comments', or with 'No comment' data at all. After duplicating the VoiceThread, and giving it a unique name, it is then open to further customization. You'll find it accessible from the 'Home' screen, and this method provides a fast and easy way to recreate content for different classes and levels of language learner, and provides a number of different options to begin to teach with VoiceThread.

12

What are the key points behind VoiceThread use in the TESOL context?

Several key points that need considering when VoiceThread technology is employed with language learning students include the following:

- Once created, VoiceThreads are immediately web-accessible. They can be embedded into other websites such as blogs, wikis, and of course learner management systems, and they can be used to provide extended learning.

- VoiceThreads are an online dependent technology. Contingency plans may be required to cover unexpected internet outage or technology breakdowns if they are being used with learners during class or work hours.

- VoiceThreads are extremely adaptable. They are useful for a multitude of purposes across a range of subject and curriculum areas, and they afford a number of opportunities to engage in online discussion while practicing speaking and writing skills asynchronously.

- Keep comments succinct. Longer comments (four or more sentences) may discourage language learners (depending on their level), and some might doubt their ability to give the kind of spoken or written comments expected by the teacher. Keep in mind that students will attempt to emulate the kind of comments that you make, and that second-language students may need to be provided with starter sentences before they are able to construct comprehensive comments.

- Become involved in student constructed VoiceThreads. Provide guidance, advice, structure, authority, and most importantly, monitor continued thread development.

- Enforce guidelines. Regulate student participation, establish a standard of quality, and hold students accountable for their online work.

- Spotlight student comments. Reinforce effective comments and highlight the areas where poor comments can be improved.

- Always safeguard students. Constantly monitor all student-created VoiceThreads for inappropriate content and comments. Protect the privacy of learners and obtain parental permission to use VoiceThreads with students if necessary.

- Address copyright, and cite resources. Any works cited or used as resources need to be mentioned in a reference list, and this can be housed in a word or pdf file that can be provided on the last slide of a VoiceThread. Keep in mind that students may also need to be taught about aspects of educational fair use as well as plagiarism.

- Evaluate with a comprehensive rubric. Take into account the two sides of student participation, with the creation, development, and end product on one side, which is the VoiceThread ultimately produced by the learner or their group, and the various comments individual students have made on other class members' VoiceThreads on the other side.

As an interactive tool that allows for collaborating, sharing, and commenting, VoiceThread has come to change the way that information can be presented, disseminated, and discussed online. Essentially, it has come to open up new possibilities that provide second-language learners and their teachers with a means to engage in visually-based asynchronous conversations in a multitude of ways, while promising to provide language learners with another way to share their voices and practice language output.

13

Lesson plan guides, and example implementation

Provided here are lesson plan guides, focusing on the use and construction of a VoiceThread, as well as an example for implementing VoiceThread in the educational context. The guides are meant to assist in the understanding of how to develop a detailed lesson plan, and to help describe what each component and stage of a lesson may cover. The example implementation is intended to provide a use-case scenario detailing the techniques required to apply the use of a VoiceThread in a real-world setting.

The content covered here includes:
- Lesson plan general guide
- Lesson plan guide for VoiceThreading in the classroom
- Example implementation: VoiceThread

Lesson Plan General Guide	
Teaching Context	
Level of Proficiency and Maturity	Student language level (e.g. beginner, intermediate, advanced). Student age range (e.g. young learners, adults).
Lesson Length	Time allotted for the class (e.g. 35-45 minutes).
Lesson Topic	Major theme or focus of the lesson (e.g. numbers and time).
Objectives	Lesson aims (e.g. to teach students how to tell the time and date accurately).
Outcomes	Learning outcomes (e.g. students will be able to read analog and digital timepieces).
Relevant Prior Learning	Anything that students need to know before starting work on this lessons' content (e.g. students need to have completed Chapter Two of the book, and have previously met language associated with appointments, calendars, and timekeeping).

Teacher Preparation	
Hardware	Types of computer or peripherals required (e.g. USB sticks, MP3 players).
Software	Name of software used (e.g. Photo Story 3, Microsoft Word).
Webpage Links	Hyperlink to web resources (e.g. www.google.com).
Additional Resources	Other necessary materials for the lesson (e.g. handouts, worksheets, textbooks).

Procedure			
Stage and Timing	**Objective**	**Teacher**	**Students**
Review Stage (if required, 5 minutes)	Focus of stage (e.g. encourage the use of previously acquired language).	Indicate what the teacher says and does in each stage of the lesson.	Provide expected examples of student behavior.

Warm-up Stage/Pre-Technology Use (10 minutes)	Focus of stage (e.g. introduce new concepts and language to students in a meaningful manner).	Indicate what the teacher says and does in each stage of the lesson.	Provide expected examples of student behavior.
Main Stage/ Technology-based Activity (20 minutes)	Focus of stage (e.g. allow students to utilize technology to become familiar with and apply the concepts and language content introduced in the lesson).	Indicate what the teacher says and does in each stage of the lesson.	Provide expected examples of student behavior.

Practice Stage (15 minutes)	Focus of stage (e.g. allow learners to utilize the skills and language that they are expected to acquire during the lesson in a practical way).	Indicate what the teacher says and does in each stage of the lesson.	Provide expected examples of student behavior.
Lesson Summation Stage/Post-Technology Activities (10 minutes)	Focus of stage (e.g. instructor reinforces the importance of language concepts and skills acquired, stating how they will be useful in forthcoming lessons).	Indicate what the teacher says and does in each stage of the lesson.	Provide expected examples of student behavior.

Further Considerations	
Follow-Up Activities	Prepare material that can be applied in a follow-up class. Also, be ready with activities for students who complete their class work earlier than expected.
Contingency Plan(s)	Always prepare an alternate teaching scenario in case of any problems. For example, a sudden power outage, or a timetabling issue could make the assigned room unavailable.
Evaluation	Reflect on what worked well, and what did not, and how you might deliver the lesson differently or improve upon it when running it again.

Lesson Plan Guide for VoiceThreading in the Classroom	
Teaching Context	
Level of Proficiency and Maturity	Beginner to advanced. Adaptable for use with young learners through to adults.
Lesson Length	Several lessons (over a week to a term). Homework completion components. Time allotted for each class: 50 minutes.
Lesson Topic	Variable, from portfolio compilation to single topic presentation.
Objectives	1. Enhance communication skills by expressing opinions on a topic, and commenting on others' topics using a variety of methods. 2. Strengthen media literacy and digital literacy skills (use software, images, audio, video, and other media elements or components).

Outcomes	1. Students will create a multimedia-based presentation.
	2. Students will employ a range of media resources during their presentation.
	3. Students will show evidence of the ability to express personal opinions on a topic, and asynchronously comment on others' topics.
Relevant Prior Learning	Students need to be familiar with using audio recording hardware, and with searching for and compiling multimedia-based resources.

Teacher Preparation	
Hardware	Computer or tablet, with internet access and microphone, camera, and scanner (if scanning resources). USB sticks or Google Drive for storage of resources if needed.
Software	Microsoft Word (if conducting any mind mapping and note-taking). VoiceThread.
Webpage Links	Flickr, Google image search, freemusicarchive.org, VoiceThread.
Additional Resources	VoiceThread creation handout; VoiceThread comment reflection extension activity handout. Both handouts can be used by students in an offline context, and can be completed during class time.

Procedure – Day 1 of 2			
Stage and Timing	Objective	Teacher	Students
Review Stage (10 minutes)	Remind students of the elements that make a good topic presentation. Reintroduce concepts of laying out a topic presentation.	Teacher elicits information from students by asking questions (e.g. what makes a good topic? How do you structure a topic presentation?), with responses to be written on the board.	Students should be able to provide several examples of how to present on a single topic, and provide some example topics.
Warm-up Stage/Pre-Technology Use (15 minutes)	Introduce a VoiceThread by using a teacher-created example.	Show an example VoiceThread with comments as a best practice model.	Students are introduced to a teacher created VoiceThread.

Main Stage (20 minutes)	Develop an initial VoiceThread with students, using the incorporating and constructing a VoiceThread for the Integration in the Classroom handout and resource notes as a guide.	Work through the development of a VoiceThread with students, helping them to develop their first VoiceThread. Introduce new vocabulary as required.	Students work with the teacher, and together, they develop an initial, very basic VoiceThread that contains two or three media artifacts and as many slides with at least one comment.
Lesson Summation Stage/Post-Technology Activities (5 minutes)	Students should be reminded of lesson goals. Individuals can highlight important VoiceThread components, and how to comment.	Remind students of lesson aims. Help them identify key elements of a VoiceThread. Homework: gather resources on a topic idea.	Students should have a good understanding of the workings of a VoiceThread, and be able to make a comment on a slide.

Procedure – Day 2 of 2			
Stage and Timing	**Objective**	**Teacher**	**Students**
Review Stage (10 minutes)	Remind students of their homework, and check that it has been completed.	Teacher ensures that students have collected a variety of resources on a topic (including images, music, and notes).	Students have prepared images to use in a VoiceThread that will present a topic of their choice.
Warm-up Stage/Pre-Technology Use (10 minutes)	The VoiceThread creation handout can be introduced to students.	The teacher works offline with students to help them lay out the structure of their VoiceThread using an associated handout.	Students complete the handout with focus on the aims and goals associated with the development of their VoiceThread and topic.

Main Stage (20 minutes)	Students begin to use the VoiceThread tool to develop and finalize their topic.	The teacher assists students in the development of their VoiceThreads, placing and uploading of media artifacts and in making comments on each slide.	Students successfully sequence their topic presentation using a variety of media artifacts and making a number of comments (at least one per slide).
Lesson Summation Stage/Post-Technology Activities (10 minutes)	Students should have finalized their VoiceThread presentation, or the majority of it, with tidying up and peer commenting set as homework.	Ensure students have successfully completed their VoiceThread, and are ready for peers to comment on it. They should be ready to comment on others.	Students complete their VoiceThread, and share it so that class peers can leave a comment on it for homework.

Further Considerations	
Follow-Up Activities	The VoiceThread comment reflection extension activity handout can be used in a follow-up lesson to help prompt students' thinking regarding the comments left on their VoiceThread by their peers. It can also serve as a means to evaluate how the use of VoiceThread has gone over with your students, and what areas could be improved with a future implementation.
Contingency Plan(s)	The use of the handout used in Warm-Up Stage/Pre-Technology use on Day 2 can be extended, and used to fill a full class hour. However, if this is not used at this time, then the next lesson in the course syllabus should be ready in case there is a problem with using the VoiceThread website or any other technology.
Evaluation	What are the biggest frustrations for implementation? Can these be remedied next time? What are the successes of the lesson? What did students get out of this activity? Can more language practice be provided?

Example Implementation:
VoiceThread

The Teaching and Learning Context

VoiceThreads are an effective way for all students, at any language level, to begin practicing speaking. VoiceThread development also allows for the practice of a variety of computer-based skills alongside language practice, and offer students the ability to listen and go over content as many times as they wish before having to share it with their peers, the teacher, or other stakeholders. For students then, it can serve as a tool that allows them to share their ideas, listen to others and respond by talking; for teachers it can serve as a means of providing assessment that can be easily moderated and graded, as all work is distributed in a central location. Essentially, VoiceThreads can provide every student with a voice, and every student the ability to comment, after being able to think through what it is that they want to say and present.

Teaching Material

The teaching material can be broken down into three: the software, the hardware, and the tasks and activities behind the learning content.

The software

The software is the VoiceThread application, depending on device used, or the VoiceThread website accessible through any browser. The software is intuitive enough for a broad range of learners to be able to become familiar with it in a short time frame, and be able to embed content, comment, and share easily.

The hardware

The hardware is a device capable of accessing the VoiceThread website or using the VoiceThread application, and has a built-in microphone (for voice comments) or web camera (for video comments). The device should have the ability to work with the documents that can be imported into a VoiceThread as well, including image files (such as, JPG), Microsoft

PowerPoint and Word files, PDF files, and video files (like MP4).

The learning content

Due to the flexibility behind the types of documents that a VoiceThread can house, and the means of providing comments on them, the learning content will vary on an activity-to-activity basis. It will, however, reflect the content that students are working on during class or for homework.

Procedure

As with a lot of technology use in the classroom, it may prove best to use one item per term or semester, so that students can become familiar with it and complete all their assignments or tasks when using it. This could prove especially the case with a site like VoiceThread, where students can comment using a variety of modes (by recording audio or video, or by typing or annotating), and use it to showcase a variety of media. To this end, a number of potential activities are introduced to illustrate the range of ideas that can be applied to the use of VoiceThread in the TESOL setting. The ideas presented here are provided as examples, and are meant to illustrate how a VoiceThread can be adapted and applied to learning. Ultimately, you will need to decide how best to adapt and implement activities from your classes to the world of VoiceThread. The challenge will be to ensure that all students are able to record their voice or response so that it is clear and audible to all.

Week one – TeacherThreads

To start students out with VoiceThreading, it is a good idea to create a sample thread which can be used to show students how to embed content, and the various means of how to comment on that content. In this way, the first VoiceThread is used as a tutorial and for practice where students become familiar with how to view, use, and comment on the site and the application. It serves as an icebreaker to the tool.

Week two – StudentThreads

The second VoiceThread should be a short VoiceThread created by the students themselves. If each student works solo, then you can discover where problems for each individual might reside, be they technical or linguistic. Alternatively, students working in groups can help each other solve any technical problems or any other issues that might arise, but this may see the more challenged students not able to produce their own VoiceThreads at a later date.

Week three – ActivityThreads

VoiceThreads can then focus on aspects of content including vocabulary, pronunciation, and writing. Assignments should now become ones where students create their own VoiceThreads, working by themselves or with peers, upload them, share them with the class, and begin to comment on the material. Of course, teacher-initiated VoiceThreads and prompts can also be used to target specific areas or use of required content in a variety of different ways. Several example activities are included here.

BookThread

Students can use VoiceThread as a presentation medium to provide a book review, with other students giving their opinion on the book in the comments. Students can upload an image of the book, or they can develop a book trailer as part of their presentation. This could follow on from a digital storytelling project or from a WebQuest on book trailers.

DirectionsThread

Students can provide a map of their route to school, or how to get to one of their favorite places from school. This could link to a unit on directions.

EssayThread

Students can either upload their entire essay as a file for others to read and then comment on. For shorter essays, students can provide the text and read it aloud, and other students can then provide spoken or written feedback on the work.

PreviewThread

Each week, a VoiceThread could be used to introduce the class topic, with specific questions set to have students think about the topic, or to answer using set phrases or expressions. This may lead to more students willing to respond in class, as they have already practiced using the content at home, and uploaded this to the VoiceThread before coming to class.

StoryThread

Students develop a story by responding to peer photographs with a voice comment. Each student takes a photo of something that they find interesting while on their way to school. This can be uploaded to a VoiceThread with the next student commenting on the photograph, before uploading one of his or her own, which the next student will comment upon. The teacher can provide a photograph for the first student to respond to, and the teacher can respond to the last student's photograph in order to close the story.

TestPracticeThread

A number of test practice contents can be adapted for use as part of a VoiceThread, from the International English Language Testing System (IELTS) to the Test of English for International Communication (TOEIC). For example, in TOEIC, students need to be able to predict questions regarding a photo or be able to describe a photo. In VoiceThread, students can be presented with a photograph, and they can leave a comment to describe it. This also gives students the chance to practice their pronunciation, intonation, grammar, vocabulary, and the cohesiveness of their description, all of which are points examined during the speaking component of the TOEIC.

TextBookThread

Any page from a textbook can be uploaded into a VoiceThread for students to comment on, and this can include providing a picture and inviting brainstorming on a topic, uploading text that students need to provide an opinion on, and delivering a cloze exercise where each student has to speak the completed sentence as a comment (with enough sentences for students to record one comment each).

TongueTwisterThread

Each student can be asked to make a voice comment while having to read a series of tongue twisters. This provides teachers with a means of quickly assessing the pronunciation skills of all students, and provides them with the means to practice pronunciation and to hear their peers' pronunciation.

Example tongue twisters include:
- Lovely Lucy loves lucky Larry.
- She sells seashells by the seashore.
- How much wood would a woodchuck chuck if a woodchuck could chuck wood?
- Red rabbits rush to the right really rudely.
- Red leather, yellow leather.
- Peter Piper picked a pack of pickled peppers.
- Thirty-three thieves rushed through the thick thorny thicket last Thursday.

TutorialThread

Students can illustrate how they use various tools, like Daum Maps (map.daum.net) or Google Maps (maps.google.com), to get to specific places, and this can match to a lesson on directions or to a lesson on travel. These kinds of VoiceThreads can also demonstrate how to perform specific tasks with students uploading demonstration videos. Students could show others how to prepare and cook their favorite dish while providing the recipe, and this can link to a lesson on food or shopping. If the setting allows, the food could then be brought to a final class party.

VideoResponseThread

The teacher can post a video to a VoiceThread, such as a short TedTalk or a silent short film, and students can respond to it. If a TEDTalk is used, students can either respond to specific questions or comment about something interesting or new that they have learned while watching the video. If a silent short film is used, then students can comment on the sequence of events, if the task is to practice this kind of language.

14
Photocopiable material

This section of the book contains photocopiable handouts, and you can feel free to make as many copies as you require for teaching purposes and for use within your classes. Any other use or distribution should include a citation to the source of the content.

Providing students with a handout to use during development of their VoiceThreads is essential, as it can help guide them in the development of their project, as well as the media resources that they may ultimately wish to select to accompany it. Two guides are provided here, one designed primarily for teacher use and the other oriented toward student use. Providing such a guide to students in the classroom allows them to start thinking about the ideas behind their VoiceThread without actually being tied to the use of technology. To augment these two guides, the VoiceThread comment reflection extension activity handout can then be used to prompt students' thinking on comments, or used in a follow-up lesson centering on a discussion of the comments that were left on the VoiceThreads. It can also serve as a means to evaluate how the use of VoiceThread has gone over with your students, and what areas can be improved with a future implementation. The handout can be used as is, but it will likely need modification to meet the needs of your specific students and teaching context, particularly if you are working with young learners. In any case, the aim of the comment reflection handout is to enable leaners to identify and record items of interest, factors they agreed or disagreed with, things that changed their thinking, elements that challenged them, and along with language learning outcomes (such as new vocabulary or expressions that they were able to employ or pick up), things they learned while engaging in VoiceThread use.

Also provided is a lesson plan template that can be used for considering how best to integrate the steps for using VoiceThread with classes. As such, the template is meant to act as means to begin thinking about how to implement, with your classes, aspects of what has been discovered through this book. The template should be supplemented with any necessary material, along with the staging as well as other aspects of the lesson being adjusted as required.

The following photocopiable material is available:

- Incorporating and constructing a VoiceThread for integration into the classroom resource notes
- VoiceThread creation resource notes
- VoiceThread creation handout
- VoiceThread comment reflection extension activity resource notes
- VoiceThread comment reflection extension activity
- Lesson plan template

Incorporating and Constructing a VoiceThread for Integration into the Classroom Resource Notes

VoiceThread goal

State the learning outcome or the intended direction of the VoiceThread below.

Intended direction

Explicitly express the educational focus or aim behind the VoiceThread here.

Learning outcome(s): State the primary learning objective here. State the secondary, or any other, learning objective(s) here.

Potential media artifacts

List artifacts by type, and describe the rationale behind how each meets the intended direction of the VoiceThread and any desired learning outcome(s).

Documents

List all the artifacts required to create the VoiceThread.

Document rationale: List how each artifact meets the VoiceThread direction or learning outcome(s)

Images

List all the images necessary for the VoiceThread.

Image rationale: List how each image meets the VoiceThread direction or a learning outcome(s).

Video   List all the video required for the VoiceThread.   *Video rationale:* List how each video meets the VoiceThread direction or learning outcome(s).
Model comments   Write out some ideas for initial comments per slide, expand as necessary, and determine the best format.   *Slide 1 comment type*   Voice, typed, uploaded audio, webcam, narration.   *Comment:* Draft comments here.   *Slide 2 comment type*   Voice, typed, uploaded audio, webcam, narration.   *Comment:* Draft comments here.   *Slide 3 comment Type*   Voice, typed, uploaded audio, webcam, narration.   *Comment:* Draft comments here.
Notes   Make any additional notes here.

VoiceThread Creation Resource Notes

VoiceThread Title	Group Members
A title is chosen by students, and written here.	Student names are listed here.

Slide Number

Write the slide number being worked on here.

Media Resources (choice of media and why)	Focus (aim/goal/learning outcome)	Comment (format and wording)
Sketch an example to reflect what will appear on this slide of your VoiceThread. Keep in mind that the document, image, or video that you select must match the comments that you will make regarding it, and align with the focus or goal that you are trying to communicate.	What are you trying to communicate or achieve with your VoiceThread – is there an intended learning outcome? What is the aim or goal of your VoiceThread?	What format will your comment take? (Consider voice-only, webcam, use of the notation tool). What comment will you leave on this slide? (Write out your comment here).

VoiceThread Creation Handout

VoiceThread Title	Group Members

Slide Number

Media Resources (choice of media and why)	Focus (aim/goal/learning outcome)	Comment (format and wording)

Slide Number

Media Resources (choice of media and why)	Focus (aim/goal/learning outcome)	Comment (format and wording)

VoiceThread Comment Reflection
Extension Activity Resource Notes

VoiceThread Title		Student Names
A title is chosen by students, and written here.		Student names are listed here.
Reflection Questions	**Example**	**Reason**
What comment(s) did you find particularly interesting?	Write the comment(s) here.	State what made the comment(s) interesting.
What comment(s) did you particularly agree with?	Write the comment(s) here.	State why you agree with the comment(s).
What comment(s) did you particularly disagree with?	Write the comment(s) here.	State why you disagree with the comment(s).
What comment(s) made you change the way that you think?	Write the comment(s) here.	State how your thinking changed.
What was the most challenging aspect of VoiceThread for you?	Write the aspect(s) here.	State your reason(s) here.
What new vocabulary or expression(s) did you learn?	Write the new term(s) here.	Write the meaning(s) here.
What other thing(s) did you learn when using VoiceThread?	Write the other thing(s) learned here.	How did you learn about the thing(s) listed?

VoiceThread Comment Reflection Extension Activity		
VoiceThread Title		**Student Names**
Reflection Questions	**Example**	**Reason**
What comment(s) did you find particularly interesting?		
What comment(s) did you particularly agree with?		
What comment(s) did you particularly disagree with?		
What comment(s) made you change the way that you think?		
What was the most challenging aspect of VoiceThread for you?		
What new vocabulary or expressions did you learn?		
What other thing(s) did you learn when using VoiceThread?		

Lesson Plan Template

Teaching Context	
Level of Proficiency and Maturity	
Lesson Length	
Lesson Topic	
Objectives	
Outcomes	
Relevant Prior Learning	
Teacher Preparation	
Hardware	
Software	
Webpage Links	
Additional Resources	

Procedure			
Stage and Timing	Objective	Teacher	Students
Review Stage (if required)			
Warm-up Stage/Pre-Technology Use			
Main Stage/ Technology-based Activity			
Practice Stage			
Lesson Summation Stage/Post-Technology Activities			

Further Considerations	
Follow-Up Activities	
Contingency Plan(s)	
Evaluation	

15

Resources list

As sites continuously go down, merge, and emerge, perhaps only a small selection of all appropriate resource content should be presented here. An attempt at keeping the number of resources to a select few for each type also provides a sample that is both comprehensive and extensive, but not overwhelming. Like any other instructor resource list, individuals will be able to add to the content as they find material that is useful, creating their own bookmark list, and over time, come to curate a vast resource library tailored to their individual teaching and learning context. Each section of this list is broken down into applications that are mostly all freely available for use with Android or iOS devices, computers, or web-based platforms.

Teachers who wish to make notes, or to record any additional resources that they come across, can use the notes section at the end of this chapter.

The following content is covered:

- App creation
- Audio creation/editing
- Blogs
- Bookmarking
- Books
- Coding
- Comic strip generators
- Copyright
- Digital story creation
- Image resources
- Image editing
- Interactive whiteboards
- Mashups
- Media timelines
- Music resources
- Podcasting
- Podcatchers
- Presentations
- Publishing
- QR codes
- Rubrics
- Screencasting
- Storyboarding and scripting
- Story creation apps
- Video editing
- Video resources
- WebQuests
- Wikis

App Creation

Android – n/a

iOS – n/a

Computer – n/a

Web

Android Creator [free/paid] creates free Android apps without the need for programming knowledge.

AppMakr [free/paid] is a template based application creator that relies on drag and drop of elements for the development of no-coding required applications. It is available in a variety of languages.

Appy Pie [free/paid] relies on templates as well as drag and drop for users to begin creating their app. It requires no coding skills.

AppYourself [paid] is an app creation tool aimed at the business market.

Como DIY [paid] is a do-it-yourself app creation tool aimed to mostly target to businesses, and is available in a number of languages.

iBuildApp [paid] is a template driven app creator for iPhone and Android phones.

Audio Creation/Editing

Android

PCM Recorder [free] is a simple voice recorder.

Pocket WavePad [free] records edits and adds effects to audio.

TapeMachine [paid] is a graphical sound recorder and editor.

iOS

Pocket WavePad [free] records edits and adds effects to audio.

Voice Memos [paid] is voice recorder that allows multitasking.

Computer

Audacity [free] is an open source digital editing program available for Mac and PC which you can use to record, edit and mix narration and music.

Pocket WavePad [free] records, edits, and adds effects to audio for Mac.

GoldWave [free/paid] is a digital audio editor that provides simple recording as well as more sophisticated processing, restoration, enhancement, and conversion for Windows and Linux. A free version is available for evaluation purposes, after which a lifetime license can be purchased.

Web

Twistedwave [free] is a browser-based audio editor that can record or edit any audio file.

Blogs

Android

> **Blogaway** [free] is a simple application to allow blogging on-the-go. It works with Blogger and allows for post creation, adding of photos, videos, multiple account management, saving of drafts, bookmarking, and a host of formatting options.

iOS

> **Disqus** [free] is a commenting system that can be included in blogs as an add-on. The application provides an easy way to moderate comments and publish responses to keep engagement levels high.

> **TravelPod – Travel Blog** [free] is a blogging application that works on- and offline, and is designed to be used while traveling.

Computer – n/a

Web

> **Blogger.com** [free] will host your blog for free, and aside from being very easy to use, it allows some level of privacy so it can be suitable for use as a class blogging site. From a single account, you can create as many blogs as you wish and determine who is allowed to comment on the content.

BuzzSumo [paid] allows users to search for blog posts that have been highly shared across social media.

Edublogs.org [free] allows teachers to create and mange their own and students' websites. There is room for customization of design and the ability to add various media to this private and secure platform.

Kidblog.org [free] is an easy-to-use, safe, and secure publishing platform designed for students in grades K-12. There are a number of excellent features including privacy and password protection, and there is no need for student personal information to be collected, nor is there any advertising. It is free for up to fifty students per class.

WordPress.org [free] is one of the most popular blogging platforms in use today as it is open-source and is easily customizable. The downloadable software for self-hosting purposes is much more flexible than that available on the blogging platform.

Twitter [free] deserves a mention here as it is useful for microblogging (posting short frequent updates). It allows users to post and read short 140-character posts called 'tweets'.

Tumblr [free] is a blogging platform open to those over thirteen years of age, with most users using pen names over their real names when blogging. Users can post on their blog, follow others, and search posts. It is unique in that posts are divided into media types: text, photo, quote, link, chat, audio, and video.

Bookmarking

Android

Bookmark [free] is a cross-platform app that allows for the syncing of bookmarks across different browsers and devices.

Delicious [free] provides users with the ability to organize links to content on the internet that they would like to save, the ability to discover links, edit tags and comments, and also to explore content saved by friends.

Facebook Save [free] is a built-in option for saving Facebook news content to read at a later date.

Instapaper [free] provides an offline archiving solution for web pages, and it presents this content to be read in newspaper fashion. Content can be highlighted, and notes can be added while reading.

Pinterest [free] allows users to pin posts (for example, web pages, images, and videos) and organize them around a common theme.

Pocket [free] integrates with a large number of third party applications that allow for the building of bookmarks. Web pages, videos, images, and whatever else can be used offline for bookmarking. Archiving maintains the links but removes the content from offline availability.

iOS

Delicious [free] allows users to save content from the internet (including web pages, blog posts, tweets, pictures, and video), and provides options for searching through others' collections of links.

Facebook Save [free] is a built-in option for saving Facebook news content to read at a later date.

Instapaper [free] provides an offline archiving solution for web pages and presents this content to be read in newspaper fashion. Content can be highlighted, and notes can be added while reading.

Pinterest [free] allows users to pin posts (for example, web pages, images, and videos) and organize them around a common theme.

Pocket [free] integrates with a large number of third party applications that allow for the building of bookmarks. Web pages, videos, images, and whatever else can be used offline for bookmarking. Archiving maintains the links but removes the content from offline availability.

Computer

EdwinSoft's UltimateDemon [paid] is link building software that helps to provide search engine optimization to a website.

Pinterest [free] allows users to pin posts (for example, web pages, images, and videos) and organize them around a common theme.

Pocket [free] integrates with a large number of third party applications that allow for the building of bookmarks. Web pages, videos, images, and whatever else can be used offline for bookmarking. Archiving maintains the links but removes the content from offline availability.

ReadKit [trial/paid] offers an Apple Mac curative and archiving platform for the content found in your other bookmarking applications (like Pocket and Instapaper) and RSS readers, and provides an extra level of organization to this content.

Web

Delicious [free] is a social bookmarking site that allows users to bookmark webpages to the internet instead of locally.

Facebook Save [free] is a built-in option for saving Facebook news content to read at a later date.

Instapaper [free] provides an offline archiving solution for web pages, and it presents this content to be read in newspaper fashion. Content can be highlighted, and notes can be added while reading.

OnlyWire [paid] works with WordPress and offers automatic submission of content to social networking and social bookmarking sites.

Pocket [free] integrates with a large number of third party applications that allow for the building of bookmarks. Web pages, videos, images, and whatever else can be used offline for bookmarking. Archiving maintains the links but removes the content from offline availability.

Books

Android

Wattpad Free Books [free] provides access to free stories and books written by aspiring authors.

iOS

Free Books – Ultimate Classics Library [free] features free access to 23,469 classic books.

Computer – n/a

Web

BookRix [free] allows access to thousands of books to read either online or to download as ebooks.

Children's Storybooks Online [free] provides a series of illustrated stories for all ages to read.

Coding

Android

Run Marco! [free] offers users the opportunity to play an adventure game while they learn to code. The application presents instructions using 'Blocky', which is the same as that used by the official Hour of Code tutorials.

Tynker [free] is an easy way for children to learn programming skills as they solve puzzles to learn concepts and build games, or control robots and drones. A number of templates are available for free.

iOS

Codea [paid] is a software development tool that uses the Lua programming language to teach users how to program.

Hopscotch [free] is an application that allows users to begin learning to code by making games similar to Angry Birds, and sharing them so others can play them.

ScratchJr [free] allows users to program their own interactive stories and games by snapping together graphical programming blocks. The application was inspired by the Scratch programming language.

Tynker [free] is an easy way for children to learn programming skills as they solve puzzles to learn concepts and build games, or control robots and drones. A number of templates are available for free.

Computer

Scratch [free] allows users to create stories, games, and animations using the Scratch programming language, and then share these with others. It is a project of the Lifelong Kindergarten Group at the MIT Media Lab.

Lightbot – Programming Puzzles [paid] is an OS X game-based application that allows players to use programming logic to solve levels. The app is also available for Android and iOS devices.

Web – n/a

Comic Strip Generators

Android

> *Comic Maker* [free] creates comics from the photo gallery.
>
> *Comic Strip It! Lite* [free] takes photos or use photo gallery images to create a comic.

iOS

> *Comic Life 3* [paid] turns photos into comic pages, or creates an entire comic from scratch using templates to build pages with speech balloons, comic lettering, and photo filters.
>
> *ToonTastic* [free] is a wizard-based animated comic or cartoon creator.
>
> *Strip Designer* [paid] is software for comic creation that uses camera, library, or Facebook photo options to create a comic.

Computer

> *Comic Creator* [paid] is a basic template driven comic creator for use on a Windows computer.

Web

Pixton [free/paid] is an easy to use comprehensive online comic creator that supports narration, and offers a range of signup options from a free fun option to paid educator/business accounts.

MakeBeliefsComix [free] is a basic comic creator that uses black and white images over a four-panel comic strip. An iOS version is also available.

Toonlet [free] allows for anyone to create their own cartoon characters and web comics.

Toondoo [free] allows for the drag and drop creation of comic strips. An iOS version is also available.

Copyright

Android – n/a

iOS – n/a

Computer – n/a

Web

Creative Commons Licenses [free] gives detailed information regarding the various types of licensing afforded to creative commons, and the permissions that each license grants for the use specific works.

Image Codr [free] can assist learners and teachers alike in determining how a Flickr image can be used (as determined by the original photographer), and provides users with an automatically generated Creative Commons citation regarding the images use within digital projects.

Digital Story Creation

Android

Com-Phone Story Maker [free] combines audio, photos, and text to create stories while allowing for three different layers of audio.

WeVideo [free] is a web-based video editor that can mix images, text, video, and audio.

iOS

30hands [free] creates a story by adding narration to photos.

Magisto [free] uses a wizard to create a short video based on provided images or video content.

Splice [free/paid] combines photos, videos, music and narrations. Effects and transitions can be added.

WeVideo [free] is a web-based video editor that can mix images, text, video, and audio.

Computer

iMovie [paid] provides video creation and editing software that can create easily shareable content on a Mac. An iOS version is available.

Microsoft Photo Story 3 [free] for Windows lets you create slideshows from a wizard that includes audio, narration, and images.

Windows Movie Maker [free] for Windows operating systems is a video editing software application that allows for narration, audio, images, and video to be mixed and edited, and it comes with transitions and special effects.

Web

Animoto [paid] allows users to submit songs, choose a theme, add their photos, videos, and text to create a digital story that they can share.

Meograph [free] is a digital storytelling tool that relies on Google Earth to create map-based and timeline-based narrated stories.

WeVideo [free] is a web-based video editor that can mix images, text, video, and audio.

Image Resources

Android – n/a

iOS – n/a

Computer – n/a

Web

Cagle Cartoons [free] provides access to a number of political cartoons from around the world. The images are organized by topic with artists categorized by country.

Flickr Creative Commons [free] provides images that can be used for almost any educational project, as long as proper citation is followed

FreeFoto.com [free] has a photos area that is available under three licensing options: recognition, Creative Commons, and commercial.

Morguefile [free] provides a range of images that are copyright free, and are available for use with few or no restrictions.

Pics4Learning.com [free] is a website that provides safe and free images for educational uses. Images here are copyright-friendly and can be used for classrooms, multimedia projects, websites, videos, portfolios, or other projects.

PicSearch [free] allows you to search the internet for images, but be aware that the image may not be copyright-free, or that it may require permission to be used in projects or in any other educational contexts.

The Library of Congress Prints & Photographs Online Catalog [free] makes an attempt to ensure that as many of their images as possible are available online in a digital format.

Wikimedia [free] serves as a point from where all the images and video posted in Wikipedia can be viewed. Most of the images found here are either copyright-free or free for use with minimal restrictions.

Image Editing

Android

PicSay [free] can edit photos, overlay titles, and add special effects.

FX Camera [free] is a photo booth app that allows users to add various effects to photographs.

iOS

PhotoPad [free] can create, edit, and save vector illustrations. It can also work with photo library images.

ScreenChomp [free] allows you to share, explain, and markup images.

Computer

PhotoPad [paid] is an image editor for OS X.

PaintShop Pro [paid] is a comprehensive image editing package for Windows.

Web

Adobe Photoshop CC [paid] is a comprehensive cloud-based image editing package.

Phixr [free] is an online photo editor with various filters and effects, and it can connect to various social media sites.

FotoFlexer [free] is an online image editor offering a number of effects, distortions, and other features.

Pixlr [paid] is a comprehensive online photo editing app.

Interactive Whiteboards

Android

ExplainEverything [free] allows users to share their content by using an interactive screencasting whiteboard.

Interactive Whiteboard [free] is a virtual whiteboard that can be used for drawing or teaching various concepts as it allows for multiple finger input, straight line drawing mode, drawing move mode, and various other features.

PPT and Whiteboard Sharing [free] provides a way to share presentations, videos, and drawings in various settings including the classroom, the boardroom, and online meetings.

Whiteboard: Collaborative Draw [free] is a collaborative drawing application that allows real-time painting.

iOS

Doceri [trial/paid] combines screencasting, desktop control, and an interactive whiteboard in one application, with control through Airplay or through Mac or PC.

Educreations Interactive Whiteboard [free] is an interactive whiteboard and screencasting tool that allows annotation, animation, and narration of a number of content types.

Screenchomp [free] allows users to annotate pictures or to use the application as a whiteboard. Any work completed with the application can be saved automatically to the internet.

ShowMe Interactive Whiteboard [free] allows voice-over recording of whiteboard interactions so that tutorials can be created easily before being shared online.

Computer

Open Sakore [free] is open-source and it is dedicated to teacher and student use. It allows for insertion of multiple document types, along with annotation capabilities for commenting drawing and highlighting content.

Smoothboard Air [free] is a collaborative interactive whiteboard for multiple iPads and for Android tablets. It allows users to annotate desktop applications wirelessly through the use of a web browser.

Web

A Web Whiteboard [free] is a online whiteboard application that allows a number of devices (like computers, tablets, and smartphones), to draw sketches, and to collaborate with others around the globe.

Realtime Board [free] is a whiteboard in a browser that allows for collaboration among a number of users.

Twiddla [free] is a web-based meeting environment that allows users to mark up photos, graphics, and websites, or to just start out with a blank canvas.

Web Whiteboard [free] is a simple way to draw and write together online by creating an online whiteboard with a click, and sharing it live or by sending the link to others.

Mashups

Android

> ***Edjing 5 DJ Music Mixer*** [free] not only transforms any android device into a turntable, but it provides access to a range of music libraries.

iOS

> ***iMashup*** [paid] is a professional quality remixing app that allows users to create their own mashups and remixes.

> ***Pacemaker*** [free] allows users to create and save mixes on an iPhone or iWatch, and to DJ live from iPad devices.

Computer

> ***Mixxx*** [free] is an advanced open source DJ package that includes an extensive array of features for OS X and Windows.

Web

> ***Mashstix*** [free] is a website with user submitted mashups available.

Media Timelines

Android

> *RWT Timelines* [free] allows students to create a graphical representation of any event or process by displaying items sequentially along a line. The final product can be exported as a pdf, or saved to the device's camera roll.

> *Timeline* [free] allows users to create timelines and associate them with colors, and to view multiple timelines together. It is a useful reference tool for remembering dates.

iOS

> *TimelineBuilder* [paid] allows users to create custom timelines with images and text with unique beginning and end dates.

> *Timeline Maker* [free] provides an easy way to display a series of events in a chronological order.

Computer

> *Edraw Timeline Maker* [paid] is a tool that makes it simple to create a professional looking timeline, history, schedule, time table, or project plan diagram from scratch.

TimelineMaker [paid] provides a simplified timeline charting tool aimed at project planners, and business professionals, and those in educational contexts.

Web

Capzles [free] allows users to create rich multimedia experiences from videos, photos, music, blogs, and documents by integrating these into a timeline of sequential events, and then share them on various social media platforms.

Hstry [free] is specifically designed for the education sector, and it allows teachers and students to create interactive timelines for assignments and online sharing.

OurStory [free] offers a means for creating story-based timelines with pictures.

Timeline [free] from *readwritethink* allows students of all ages to easily create a graphical representation of related items or events in sequential order and display them along a line using various images and text.

TimeGlider [free] is a web-based timeline project creator that allows zooming and panning across timelines. Users are able to set the size of events as they relate to importance.

Tiki-Toki [free/paid] is a web-based timeline editor that allows viewing of timelines in 3D, and it allows for the integration of images and videos.

WhenInTime [free] is a web application for creating and sharing media-based timelines.

Music Resources

Android

> *FindSounds* [free] can be used to search the internet for sounds that can then be saved as ringtones, notifications, or alarms.

> *Shazam* [free] allows Android device users to identify the music playing around them, as well as discover song lyrics, and other music related information and tracks.

iOS

> *Shazam* [free] allows iOS device users to identify the music playing around them, as well as discover song lyrics, and other music related information and tracks.

Computer – n/a

Web

> *300 Monks* [free] provides a comprehensive source of royalty free music.

> *ccMixter* [free] is a free music site that is community based and promotes a remix culture. *A cappella* and remix tracks licensed under Creative Commons are available for download and use in creative works.

FMA (Free Music Archive) [free] provides access to a range of free music based on a wide variety of genre. The music is offered free under various licenses for use.

Find Sounds [free] is a long-running service that can be used to search the internet for various sounds that can then be incorporated into various projects.

FreePlay Music [free] is a service that searches the internet for free music that can be used in YouTube videos and other projects.

Podcasting

Android

Podomatic Podcast & Mix Player [free] provides access to a wide variety of podcasts, listening in offline mode, and features such as a dynamic social feed so you can see the podcasts Facebook friends follow and like.

iOS

PodOmatic Podcast Player [free] provides access to a wide variety of podcasts, listening in offline mode, and features such as a dynamic social feed so you can see the podcasts Facebook friends follow and like.

Computer

Audacity [free] is a free multi-track audio recorder and editor with some very powerful features that include those for adding effects to files and conducting analysis of the audio recorded.

iTunes [free] offers media on demand and a way to organize and enjoy music, movies, and TV shows, as well as accessing and subscribing to podcasts and screencasts.

LoudBlog [free] is a Content Management System (CMS) for podcasts. This program automatically generates skinnable websites and RSS-feeds for audio and video podcasts, including provision for show notes and links.

PodcastGenerator [free] is an open source content management system for podcast publishing. It provides a comprehensive range of tools to manage all aspects of podcast publishing.

PodProducer [free] allows for the recording of voice and the adding of effects.

Web

ESLPod [free] provides a range of podcast content tailored to second-language learners of English from specific topics through to test-taking guides.

FeedForAll [free] allows for the creation, editing, and publishing of RSS feeds.

Feedity [free] is an online tool for creating an RSS feed for any web page, with an option to upgrade to a premium account that offers additional features.

FETCHRSS: RSS Generator [free] is an online RSS feed generator, that can create a feed out of almost any web page, automatically updates the RSS feed when new content is added to the web page, and generates an RSS for a social networking site.

OPML Viewer [free] allows users to view the contents of outline processor markup language (OPML) files.

Podcast Alley [free] is the place to go if you are interested in podcasts, want to gain access to the top podcasts, and want to find out the latest news about podcasts.

Pod Gallery [free] is a podcasting website where podcasters can share their episodes, and where listeners can subscribe.

QT-ESL Podcasts [free] provides a range of podcasts that cover oral grammar practice and includes scripts and worksheets.

SoundCloud [free] is a social sound platform where anyone is able to create and share audio.

Podcatchers

Android

Podcast Player [free] provides a range of podcast discovery options and tools, along with a range of features including a sleep timer, video support, intelligent silence skip and volume boost, as well as support for tablet, Chromecast, and Android Wear.

Podcast Republic [free] is an application that is ad-supported. It offers a variety of features from podcast discovery and automatic downloading through to storage management, sleep timer, and car mode. Support is also included from Chromecast and Android Wear.

Pocket Casts [paid] shows subscribed podcasts in a tile format, with easy sorting and categorization functions. Video podcast is also supported, along with auto-download and cleanup of downloaded and played episodes to save on storage space. Several features allow it to stand out, including a sleep timer as well as its cross-platform nature that grants it the ability to sync between multiple devices and mobile operating systems.

iOS

Overcast: Podcast Player [free] provides a combination of powerful audio and podcast management features. The application comes with a wide variety of features that allow it to download episodes, send notifications of new episodes, and play content offline or by streaming. It can also normalize speech levels, and speed through gaps and silence in podcasts.

Castro: High Fidelty Podcasts [free] is a simple and easy to use podcatcher. It provides a simple design with automatic episode download, dynamic storage management, along with episode streaming.

Pocket Casts [paid] shows subscribed podcasts in a tile format, with easy sorting and categorization functions. Video podcast is also supported, along with auto-download and cleanup of downloaded and played episodes to save on storage space. Several features allow it to stand out, including a sleep timer as well as its cross-platform nature that grants it the ability to sync between multiple devices and mobile operating systems.

Computer

gPodder [free] is an open source media aggregator and podcast client. It is able to store information in the cloud on which shows you have listened to, and it allows for the local installation of the client for download of content.

iTunes [free] is a comprehensive media aggregator that provides comprehensive support for media management, the audio and video playback of local media, podcast search and subscription, along with automatic downloads, syncing and streaming, and many other features.

Juice [free] is a long-standing cross platform no-frills podcast aggregator that is open source, and specifically designed to manage podcasts. Features include auto cleanup, centralized feed management, and for Windows users, accessibility options for the blind and visually impaired.

Web

Cloud Caster [free] is a web-based podcaster which works across all mobile devices. It syncs progress and playlists across platforms, and provides search and support for audio and video podcasts.

Presentations

Android

Glogster [free] allows students using an Android-based device to create online multimedia posters, or Glogs, from a combination of media types (from audio, graphic, to video), and hyperlinks.

Google Slides [free] allows Android device users with a Google account a means of creating, editing, and collaborating with others on presentations.

LinkedIn SlideShare [free] allows Android device users the ability to search and explore for a variety of presentations, infographics, and documents on topics of their interest.

Microsoft PowerPoint [free] allows users to view PowerPoint presentations on their device for free, and to make edits and changes on the go.

iOS

Glogster [free] allows students using an iOS device to create online multimedia posters, or Glogs, from a combination of media types (from audio, graphic, to video), and hyperlinks.

Google Slides [free] allows iOS device users with a Google account a means of creating, editing, and collaborating with others on presentations.

Keynote [free] is a powerful presentation app that allows users to develop comprehensive presentations with animations, transitions, and multimedia elements.

LinkedIn SlideShare [free] allows iOS device users the ability to search and explore for a variety of presentations, infographics, and documents on topics of their interest.

Microsoft PowerPoint [free] allows users to view PowerPoint presentations on their device for free, and to make edits and changes on the go.

Computer

Microsoft PowerPoint [paid] is a comprehensive presentation software application, and is perhaps the most used and recognizable.

Keynote [free] is a powerful presentation app that allows users to develop comprehensive presentations with animations, transitions, and multimedia elements.

Web

Bunkr [free] is a presentation tool that displays any online content including social media posts, images, videos, audio, articles, and files.

Glogster [free] allows students to create online multimedia posters, or Glogs, from a combination of media types (from audio, graphic, to video), and hyperlinks.

Google Slides [free] allows those with a Google account, a means of creating, editing, and collaborating with others on presentations.

LinkedIn SlideShare [free] allows users to search for presentations, infographics, documents and other items on topics of their interest.

Microsoft PowerPoint Online [free] extends the Microsoft PowerPoint experience to the web browser with OneDrive integration, and allows users to create, edit, and view files on the go.

Prezi [free] is a visually oriented presentation packaged that also allows users to upload PowerPoint slides, and customize them, or use a variety of their own images, text, audio, and video.

Slidebean [free] offers a one-click presentation development system that incorporates a variety of templates into the design of presentations.

Slides [free] is a place for creating, presenting, and sharing slide decks.

Swipe [free] allows users to share a presentation link with anyone across any device, and it allows viewers to interact with the presentation on several levels, from collaboration through to taking polls.

VoiceThread [free] allows users to import various media such as images, PowerPoints, and PDFs. It provides a means of making audio or video recordings concerning those media artifacts, and it also allows other users to reply to the initial comments, by audio or video means, as the presentation progresses.

Publishing

Android

Book Creator Free [free] offers a simple means of creating a variety of ebooks including picture books, comic and photo books, and journals and textbooks. It allows for the use of images, narration, texts, annotations and drawings.

Book Writer Free [free] is a simple book creation application that allows users to share their content with others.

My Story Builder [free] is a simple, 'suitable for children', book editor.

Scribble: Kids Book Maker [paid] is an application that allows children to write, illustrate, and publish their own comprehensive stories in a range of formations including video export. It contains a series of story starters, stickers, and backgrounds to help them work on creating stories from the start.

iOS

Book Creator Free [free] offers a simple means of creating a variety of ebooks including picture books, comic and photo books, and journals and textbooks. It allows for the use of images, narration, texts, annotations and drawings.

Creative Book Builder [paid] is a professional ebook editor and generator which can also extend the utility of ebooks through the use of a range of widgets.

Demibooks Composer Pro [free] builds interactive books with animation, audio, images, and effects.

Scribble Press – Creative Book Maker for Kids [paid] contains a series of story starters, stickers and backgrounds to help get young kids working on creating stories that can be turned into ebooks.

Computer

Android Book App Maker [paid] provides users with the ability to turn content into a flip-book app.

iBooks Author [free] provides a series of templates and styles to assist in the development of ebooks for the iBook store.

Kotobee [free] provides free software to assist in the creation of ebooks and libraries for a range of platforms.

Web

Blurb [paid] is just one of many online services that can assist in the creation of ebooks.

QR Codes

Android

> *I-nigma QR & Barcode Scanner* (free) is a versatile barcode and QR code reader that can scan a multitude of codes and share these codes as well.

> *QR Code Reader* (free) is a simple QR Code and product barcode scanner.

> *QR Droid Code Scanner* (free) is a powerful barcode, QR code, and Data Matrix scanner that offers multi-language support.

iOS

> *Bakodo – Barcode Scanner and QR Barcode Reader* (free) scans all types of QR codes and barcodes.

> *QR Reader for iPhone* (free) scans a variety of codes including QR codes and barcodes, and features auto-detect scanning.

> *QRafter – QR Code and Barcode Reader and Generator* (free) is a two-dimensional barcode scanner for iOS. Along with a variety of useful features, it can scan and generate QR codes.

Computer

CodeTwo QR Code Desktop Reader (free) allows users to scan QR codes directly from their screen onto their desktop. Users select the QR code to be read by selecting the area with a QR code using their mouse.

QR-Code Studio (free) is for Mac and Windows computers. The QR code maker software is freeware.

Web

QR Code Generator (free) creates QR codes, in a limited number of formats, for free.

QR Stuff QR Code Generator (free) creates QR codes from a various types of data such as website URLs, image files, PDF files, and so on, with static and dynamic embedding options.

The QR Code Generator (free) allows for the free scan and generation of QR codes for a variety of uses.

Rubrics

Android

Daily Rubric: Any Curriculum [free] allows teachers to create and use rubrics from their Android device. Rubrics can be designed from curriculum outcomes, or based on the pre-loaded Common Core Standards.

iOS

Easy Assessment [paid] offers a means to capture and assess performance based on custom created rubrics, scale, or criteria.

Rubrics [paid] allows instructors to track student performance and produce reports based on custom rubrics and grading options.

Computer – n/a

Web

Kathy Shrock's Guide to Everything: Assessment and Rubrics [free] provides access to a wide range of rubrics to help guide assessment of students.

iRubric [free] is a website where instructors can create their own rubrics, or they can build off those made available from other instructors.

RubiStar [free] allows instructors to create their own rubrics using templates designed for core subjects as well as art, music, and multimedia.

Screencasting

Android

AZ Screen Recorder [free] is a screen recording application that offers several features, including the ability to capture the front camera as well as screen recording. It also provides video trimming.

ilos Screen Recorder [free] is a simple application that records the screen and provides audio capture as well.

Telecine [free] is an open source application that allows screen recording through the use of overlays.

iOS

Doceri [trial/paid] combines screencasting, desktop control, and an interactive whiteboard in one application, with control through Airplay or through Mac or PC.

Educreations Interactive Whiteboard [free] is an interactive whiteboard and screencasting tool that allows annotation, animation, and narration of a number of content types.

Screenchomp [free] allows users to annotate pictures or to use the application as a whiteboard. Any work completed with the application can be saved automatically to the internet.

Computer

ilos screen recorder [free] automatically uploads content to their servers for storage and playback.

Screencast-O-Matic [free] offers fifteen minutes of recording time for free, both for screen and webcam, and allows users to save to places such as YouTube or as a video file.

TechSmith Camtasia Studio [free trial] is a comprehensive screen recording application that allows for audio and webcam capture as well as highlighting, adding media, and editing of recordings.

Web – n/a

Storyboarding and Scripting

Android

Ray Story Board [free] is a simple storyboard creator that lets users build storyboards from photos or gallery images, create multiple storyboards, and animate them using a slideshow feature.

Storyboard Studio [paid] is a mobile storyboarding writing tool that is suitable for artists and non-artists alike.

iOS

Penultimate [free] provides a natural feel of writing and sketching on paper, and connects to Evernote.

Storyboard Composer [paid] is a mobile storyboard previsualiztion composer for animators, art directors, film students, film directors, or anyone who would like to visualize their story.

Computer

FrameForge Previz Studio [paid] allows users to develop and previsualize films, TV shows, commercials, or similar projects at a professional level.

Storyboardpro [paid] is professional level software that combines drawing and animation tools with camera controls.

StoryBoard Quick Studio [paid] allows for the fast creation of storyboards with QuickShots, has a print-to-sketch feature, and comes with a series of character poses for integration into storylines.

Web

Google Docs [free] can be used, along with any note-taking or document editor, as a make-shift storyboard by integrating photos or pictures into the document to outline a process or the actions for a story. It is also available as an Android and iOS app.

StoryboardThat [free trial] offers an edition that allows educators to build diagrams, and visualize workflow. It features a drag and drop interface and an extensive image library.

Story Creation Apps

Android

StoryMaker 1 [free] provides a means of creating stories using templates and overlays, and the possibility of using audio, photos, or video.

Storehouse [free] allows users to share a collection of photos in a collage or album, or by telling a story that links the photos.

iOS

StoryKit [free] allows for the creation of an electronic storybook through the use of images, simple drawings, recording of sound, and by the addition of text.

Storyrobe [paid] makes photo-based slideshows with voice recording.

FotoBabble [free] adds audio to a photo to make a talking postcard.

Sock Puppets [free] lets users create lip-synced videos with characters. Various puppets, props, scenery, and backgrounds can be used.

Computer

> *Cartoon Story Maker 1.1* [free] is a simple program that creates 2D cartoon stories with conversations, dialogs (recorded and/or speech bubble), and various backgrounds.

> *StoryMaker* [free/trial] is game-based software that asks for parts of speech (such as nouns, verbs, adjectives), and these are then inserted into a story with sometimes comical results. Educators can edit and customize aspects of the aspects of the program for their context. Backgrounds can be imported, but character templates are built in.

Web

> *Littlebirdtales* [free] provides younger learners the ability to create digital storybooks.

> *Pixton* [free/paid] is a visual writing tool that allows users to make a comic using images, clipart backgrounds and artwork, as well as speech bubbles.

> *Storynet.org* [free] is a website that aims at connecting people to and through storytelling.

> *StoryJumper* [free] allows users to create illustrated storybooks from scratch or from existing templates.

Video Editing

Android

VideoShow – Video Editor [free] is an all-in-one video editor and slideshow producer that provides music, themes, filters, emojis, as well as text input.

VidTrim [free] is a video editor and organizer that allows the trimming, editing, and saving of videos.

VivaVideo: Free Video Editor [free] is a comprehensive video editor and movie maker that facilitates the creation of video-based stories.

WeVideo [free] is a comprehensive and easy to use video editor that can mix images, text, video, and audio.

iOS

iMovie [paid] is video creation and editing software that can create easily shareable content.

Splice [free] is a video editor that adds music and effects to images and videos with narration. It includes access to free songs, sound effects, text overlays, transitions, filters, and various editing tools.

ReelDirector II [paid] is a full-featured video editing app.

WeVideo [free] is an easy to use and comprehensive video editor that can mix audio, images, text, and audio.

Computer

Windows Movie Maker [free] is a video editing software application that allows for narration, audio, images, and video to be mixed and edited with transitions and special effects.

Web

Video Toolbox [free] is an online video editing and conversion tool.

WeVideo [free] is a comprehensive and easy to use web-based video editor that can mix images, text, video, and audio together to form a compelling story.

Video Resources

Android

TED [free] provides more than 2,000 TED talks from various people by topic and mood, and on a variety of topics.

Vimeo [free] is a variety of videos are available across a wide variety of topics and genres, with users having the ability to upload their own content as well.

YouTube [free] allows for editing and uploading of videos, where one can subscribe to various channels that offer a wide variety of videos on various topics and genres.

iOS

TED [free] provides more than 2,000 TED talks from various people by topic and mood, and on a variety of topics.

Vimeo [free] provides a variety of videos which are available across a wide variety of topics and genres. Users are able to upload their own content as well.

YouTube [free] allows for editing and uploading of videos, where once can subscribe to various channels that offer a wide variety of videos on various topics and genres.

Computer – n/a

Web

Clipcanvas [free] allows for the download of 600,000 royalty free HD and 4K video and film clips.

Mazwai [free] maintains a collection of free to use HD video clips and footage, and some unique time-lapse and slow motion video footages that are provided under the Creative Commons Attribution license if used commercially.

Motion Backgrounds for Free [free] is a place to download professional quality motion backgrounds and video footage.

Motion Elements [free] is a good source for premium stock videos, offering around 400 videos for free, as well as free After Effects templates.

Neo's Clip Archive [free] offers nearly 3,500 free video clips sorted by 25 categories free for use for personal, non-commercial purposes.

Pexels Videos [free] brings under one roof a video library of Creative Commons Zero licensed stock videos from a variety of different sources.

SaveTube [free] allows users to rip YouTube videos to their local computer in various audio or video-based formats.

Savevideo.me [free] allows users to rip videos from a variety of sites to their local computer.

TeacherTube [free] is an online resource that helps users to view and share videos, photos, audio, and documents on almost any topic.

WebQuests

Android – n/a

iOS – n/a

Computer – n/a

Web

Building a WebQuest [free] is a comprehensive overview of the template to follow when there is a need to construct a WebQuest.

Having Fun with Reading [free] is a WebQuest for college and adult level learners of English, where learners interact with texts and complete activities that promote cooperative and collaborative learning along with reading narrative comprehension skills.

Idioms in Your Pocket [free] is a WebQuest that is designed for high school and adult ESL students, and it allows them to discover the various meanings of English idioms.

OneStopEnglish WebQuests [free] provides a selection of WebQuests covering major holidays.

Pre-Writing Your WebQuest [free] provides prompts for users to complete in order to develop a WebQuest.

QuestGarden [free/paid] is a site designed by Bernie Dodge, the creator of WebQuests, for use by pre- and in-service teachers, professional developers, other educators, and those who work with them. The site provides hosting and template creation of WebQuests that then become searchable.

Using WebQuests to Teach English [free] is a WebQuest that can be used to teach teachers about WebQuests.

WebQuestDirect [free] is described as the world's largest searchable directory of WebQuest reviews.

WebQuest.Org [free] provides comprehensive information pertaining to the WebQuest model, and is run by Bernie Dodge, the creator of WebQuests.

Zunal [free/paid] is a site for educators to create, host, and then share their WebQuests with others.

Wikis

Android

EveryWiki: Wikipedia++ [free] aims to provide access to many wikis from a central application.

wikiHow [free] is the application associated with the leading how-to-guide wikiHow. It allows for searching of the wiki to find step-by-step instructions on how to complete almost any task.

iOS

Hack My Life – Life Hack Wiki [free] is an application that seeks to provide access to all possible life hacks. A life hack is a strategy or technique that can be used or adopted to allow for better time management or for getting more out of everyday activities.

Lyrically [free] offers access to a list of song lyrics curated by fans. Searches can be undertaken by track, artist, or by song, and there is support for in-app purchases.

Computer

DokuWiki [free] is a PHP based highly customizable and fully extensible wiki software platform. The advantage is that it requires no databases as all the data is stored in plain text, and for this reason, it is very popular and used by many sites. It has a variety of useful features, from locking to avoid edits through to a spam blacklist.

MediaWiki [free] is open-source and it is the wiki software used by Wikipedia. It is available in a number of languages, released under a general public license (GPL), and written in PHP: Hypertext Preprocessor (PHP) a server-side scripting language. There are many extensions and plugins available for free, including a what-you-see-is-what-you-get (WYSIWYG) editor.

Web

PBworks [free] (formerly PBwiki) is a real-time collaborative editing system with several solutions including one for educators. It offers a single workspace, where student accounts can be created without email addresses, and easy editing without the need for coding.

PmWiki [free] is a wiki tool that gives user-access control over individual pages, so they can be set for access by specific people with it being possible to set different passwords for each page. The software also allows for navigation trails through individual sections, insertion of tables, and provides a printable layout.

Wikidot [free] offers members the ability to create a wiki-based website with forums, where they can create a community, or publish and share documents and content.

Wikispaces [free] is a wiki hosting service that provides educators with a means to monitor student progress in real time and the ability to easily create projects and assign them to students, as well as editing tools and a social newsfeed.

Teacher Notes

Android

iOS

_____

_____

_____

_____

_____

_____

_____

_____

_____

_____

_____

_____

_____

_____

_____

_____

_____

_____

_____

Computer

Web

16
References

Akasha, O. (2011). Voicethread as a good tool to motivate ELLs and much more. In M. Koehler & P. Mishra (eds.), *Proceedings of Society for Information Technology & Teacher Education International Conference 2011* (pp. 3123-3127). Chesapeake, VA: Association for the Advancement of Computing in Education (AACE).

Burden, K. & Atkinson, S. (2008). Evaluating pedagogical 'affordances' of media sharing Web 2.0 technologies: A case study. In Hello! Where are you in the landscape of educational technology? *ascilite Melbourne 2008.*

Bush, L. (2009). Viva VoiceThread: Integrating a web 2.0 Tool in the additional language classroom In I. Gibson, R. Weber, K. McFerring, R. Carlsen & D. Willis (Eds.), *Proceedings of Society for Information Technology & Teacher Education International Conference 2009* (pp. 3247-3250). Chesapeake, VA: Association for the Advancement of Computing in Education (AACE).

Cassinelli, C. (2016). Voicethread. *Voicethread 4 Education*. Retrieved from http://voicethread4 education.wikispaces.com

Dyck, B. (2007). VoiceThread: Capturing and sharing student voice with an online twist. *EducationWorld*. Retrieved from http://www. educationworld.com/a_tech/columnists/dyck/ dyck019.shtml

Elwood, S. (2010). Digital storytelling: Strategies using VoiceThread. In D. Gibson & B. Dodge (Eds.), *Proceedings of Society for Information & Teacher Education International Conference* 2010 (pp. 1075-1079). Chesapeake, VA: Association for the Advancement of Computing in Education (AACE).

Ferriter, B. (2010). Voicethread. *Digitally Speaking*. Retrieved from http://digitallyspeaking. pbworks.com/Voicethread

Gillis, A., Luthin, K., Parette, H.P., & Blum, C. (2012). Using VoiceThread to create meaningful receptive and expressive learning activities for young children. *Early Childhood Education 40(4)*, 203--211.

Hacker, P. (2010). Using VoiceThread to give students a voice outside the classroom. *The Chronicle of Higher Education*. Retrieved from http://chronicle.com/blogs/profhacker/using-voicethread-to-give-students-a-voice-outside-the-classroom/26367

Hoskins Sakamoto, B. (2010). High tech ideas for low tech classrooms: VoiceThread. *Teaching Village*. Retrieved from http://www.teachingvillage.org/2010/05/23/high-tech-ideas-for-low-tech-classrooms-voicethread

Howland, J., Jonassen, D., & Marra, R. (2012). *Meaningful learning with technology, 4th ed.* Boston, MA: Pearson.

Hughes, H. (2012). Introduction to flipping the college classroom. In T. Amiel & B. Wilson (Eds.), *Proceedings of EdMedia: World Conference on Educational Media and Technology 2012* (pp. 2434-2438). Association for the Advancement of Computing in Education (AACE).

Lewis, T., Burks, B., Shumack, K., & Simmons, K. (2014). VoiceThread: Instructional improvement through objective feedback. In M. Searson & M. Ochoa (Eds.), *Proceedings of Society for Information Technology & Teacher Education International Conference 2014* (pp. 2907-2910). Chesapeake, VA: Association for the Advancement of Computing in Education (AACE).

Moore, A. J., Gillet, M. R., & Steele, M. D., (2014). Fostering student engagement with the flip. *The Mathematics Teacher 107*(6), 420-425.

Nicholsan, M. (2013). Flipping the classroom with VoiceThread discussions. In T. Bastianes & G. Marks (Eds.), *Proceedings of E-Learn: World Conference on E-Learning in Corporate, Government, Healthcare, and Higher Education* 2013 (pp. 1263-1264). Chesapeake, VA: Association for the Advancement of Computing in Education (AACE).

Pacansky-Brock, M. (2013). *How to humanize your online class with VoiceThread*. Imprint: Smashwords Edition.

Pallos, H. & Pallos, L. (2011). Evaluation of Voicethread technology to improve Japanese graduate students presentation skills in English in a blended learning environment. In S. Barton, J. Hedberg & K. Suzuki (Eds.), *Proceedings of Global Learn 2011* (p. 1078). AACE.

Pinto Pires, S. (2010). Give Voicethread to your students! *E-blahblah*. Retrieved from http://e-blahblah.com/index.php/2010/02/give-voicethread-to-your-students

Poelzer, T. (2009). VoiceThreads in the classroom. Tech it up! *Bringing Technology to the Classroom*. Thompson Rivers University. Kamloops, British Columbia. October 22 – 24, Canada.

Recchio-Demmin, B. (2009). Using VoiceThread as a tool for language learning. *Technology and Collaborative Creativity in Learning (TaCCL) Lab, University at Albany, SUNY*. Retrieved from http://tccl.rit.albany.edu/knilt/index.php/Using_VoiceThread_as_a_Tool_for_Language_Learning

Smith, J. & Dobson, E. (2009). Beyond the book: Using VoiceThread in language arts instruction. In T. Bastiaens, J. Dron & C. Xin (Eds.), *Proceedings of World Conference on E-Learning in Corporate, Government, Healthcare, and Higher Education 2009* (pp. 712-715). Chesapeake, VA: AACE. Retrieved from http://www.editlib.org/p/32538

Sun, Y., Yu, J. & Gao, F. (2013). Shared video media: A new environment to support peer feedback in second language learning. In R. McBride & M. Searson (Eds.), *Proceedings of Society for Information Technology & Teacher Education International Conference 2013*. (pp. 1746-1751). Chesapeake, VA: AACE.

Vesper, S. (2008). Voicethread examples in education. *Slideshare*. Retrieved from http://www.slideshare.net/suziea/voicethread-examples-in-education-presentation#

VoiceThread. (2016). VoiceThread LLC. Retrieved from http://www.voicethread.com

About the Book

VoiceThread firmly establishes itself as a tool that has the exciting potential to give an actual audible voice to those language students who rarely, if ever, speak the target language in class, and it does so by providing students with the means to construct visually-based digital conversations. In the light of this, the pedagogical affordances provided by asynchronous computer-mediated communication with this tool are considered, along with the types of educational VoiceThreads that are in use today. The efficacy behind VoiceThread development, with and for students, is then oriented toward the teaching of English to speakers of other languages (TESOL). This is followed by a brief overview of the instructional strategies useful when employing VoiceThread in English language learning contexts, supported by example activities and resources, and a means of evaluating the outcomes afforded through use of the tool. An overview of the techniques essential for monitoring, producing, and guiding effective VoiceThread development among language learners is also included, as well as a tutorial for getting started with the technology.

About the Author

David Kent is an Assistant Professor at the Graduate School of TESOL-MALL at Woosong University in the Republic of Korea. He has been working and teaching in Korea since 1995, and with a Doctorate of Education from Curtin University in Australia, he is a specialist in computer assisted language learning (CALL) and the teaching of English to speakers of other languages (TESOL). He has presented at international conferences, as well as published a number of peer-reviewed journal articles, books, and book chapters in his areas of specialization.

Also by David Kent

*A Loanword Approach to the Teaching of
English as a Foreign Language in Korea:*
Exploring the Effectiveness of a Multimedia Curriculum

Teaching with Technology:
Integrating Technology into the TESOL Classroom

Internet in Education:
Integrating the Internet into the TESOL Classroom

TESOL Strategy Guides
Digital Storytelling
The Prezi Presentation Paradigm
Podcasts and Screencasts
WebQuests
VoiceThreading

www.ingramcontent.com/pod-product-compliance
Lightning Source LLC
La Vergne TN
LVHW011230080426
835509LV00005B/409